Get Clear on Your Career

Lily Maestas, M.S.W.
University of California, Santa Barbara

KENDALL/HUNT PUBLISHING COMPANY
4050 Westmark Drive   Dubuque, Iowa 52002

Cover image © Julien Tromeur, 2008. Used under license from Shutterstock, Inc.

Copyright © 2009 by Kendall/Hunt Publishing Company

ISBN 978-0-7575-6142-9

All rights reserved. No part of this publication may be reproduced, stored in a retrieval system, or transmitted, in any form or by any means, electronic, mechanical, photocopying, recording, or otherwise, without the prior written permission of the copyright owner.

Printed in the United States of America
10 9 8 7 6 5 4 3 2

Contents

Introduction   v

Part I   Getting to Know YOU   1
Exercise 1: Sketching a Self-Portrait   3
Exercise 2: Exploring Your Joys   9
Exercise 3: Careers That Match Your Interests   13
Exercise 4: Who Do You Think You Are?   23
Exercise 5: Attitude! Everybody's Got One   29
Exercise 6: What Is Your Mission in Life?   31
Exercise 7: Your Heroes and Passions   33
Exercise 8: What Do You Want Out of Your Job?   35
Exercise 9: Feeling Good about Yourself   41
Exercise 10: Learning from the Past   43
Exercise 11: What Do You Do Well?   45
Exercise 12: How Do Your "Smarts" Work?   49
Exercise 13: Imagining Your Ideal Career   53
Exercise 14: Your Portrait Begins to Take Shape   57
Exercise 15: Introducing Your Professional Self   59

Part II   Researching the Job Market   61
Exercise 16: Developing Your Life Budget   63
Exercise 17: Where Are You on Your Career/Life Spectrum?   67
Exercise 18: Balancing Relationships with Careers   69

Part III   Career Exploration   73
Exercise 19: Becoming a Skilled Career Consumer   75
Exercise 20: Researching Career Possibilities   79
Exercise 21: Surfing the Net   81
Exercise 22: Exploring Your Options through People   83

Part IV   Exploring Further Education and Training   87
Exercise 23: Which Door Do You Open?   89
Exercise 24: Choosing Your Major   91
Exercise 25: Investigating Educational Possibilities   97
Exercise 26: Should You Be Your Own Boss?   99

Part V   Developing Your Marketing Tools   105
Exercise 27: Creating Résumés That Get a Response   107
Exercise 28: Correspondence That Sells   113
Exercise 29: Interviewing for Success   115

Part VI   Goal Setting and Review   119
Exercise 30: Career Planning Checklist   121
Exercise 31: Creating and Committing to Your Action Plan   123

Part I
Getting to Know YOU

In order to choose, prepare for, and gain a satisfying career, you must first have a solid idea of who you are and what you want. You will gather this information in a number of ways. Some may surprise you. The exercises in Part I of this workbook will help you identify your strengths and requirements for your ideal career. Start by brainstorming some of these things now and later you will add what you learn about yourself to a more comprehensive profile.

> *"In order to hunt for your ideal job, or even something close to your ideal job, you must have a picture of it in your head. The clearer the picture, the easier it will be to hunt for."*
> Richard Nelson Bolles, Author.

Exercise 1: Sketching a Self-Portrait

In this exercise, you will:
➤ Get a sense of what is important to you.
➤ Discover some of your strengths and needs.
➤ Learn some things that you require from your ideal career.
➤ Learn some basic terminology to establish your new career vocabulary.

Most people try to match themselves to jobs. As a result, more than 80 percent of the workforce is doing something they don't like, according to Carolee Kanchier, author of *Dare to Change Your Job—And Your Life*. What would happen if you started your career quest by examining what *you* want from a job? What would happen if you searched for a job that matched *you*? Chances are good you would thrive in this job because it would be a good fit. You would be doing work that interests you. Your job would be helping you reach your dreams and goals. You would be using the parts of your personality that are most rewarding to you. You would be doing things you do well and that are important to you. You would also thrive in your environment and work with people who energize and challenge you. You would be working in the part of the country you love, wearing your favorite clothes, making the money you want to make, and having the schedule you prefer. It would also balance with other important roles in your life. How much of this dream can you actually achieve? More than you think.

Begin your self-portrait by fleshing out the areas listed below. Try to list at least three responses to each category. Do your best, but don't sweat it. As you work through this exercise and the rest of the workbook, more ideas will surface. Add them as you go along.

Your Interests/Passions/Fascinations
What are you passionate about? What fascinates you? Think of what you do in your spare time (or what you would do if you had spare time), your hobbies, and extracurricular activities? What do you care deeply about? What causes would or do you already volunteer time in?
1.

2.

3.

Your Dreams/Goals
Big or small, it doesn't matter. What would you like to be, to do, to have?
1.

2.

3.

Barriers to Your Goals
What might block you from reaching your dreams and goals? These might be barriers that you can influence (such as fear, feelings of inadequacy, money, geography, lack of information, or lack of connections with the "right people"). They might be factors we have no control over (such as age, height, family responsibilities, or physical disabilities).
1.

2.

3.

Overcoming Barriers
What are some ways you can overcome your barriers. This might be talking out feelings with a friend, getting training, getting a loan, talking with or reading about those who have attained goals similar to yours, and so forth.
1.

2.

3.

Values
What is most important to you in your life? (Family, faith, independence, security, fun …)
1.

2.

3.

Current Life Roles
What are the roles in your life right now that are important to you and/or in which you spend much time and energy? (Friend, student, partner, athlete, artist, parent, child…)
1.

2.

3.

Preferred Future Life Roles
In the future, which roles in your life do you want to be important to you? (Spouse, parent, community leader, role model, traveler, lifelong friend, provider…)
1.

2.

3.

Personality
What are the strengths of your personality? What positive qualities do others notice about you? (Patient, social, organized, fun …)
1.

2.

3.

Skills
What can you do well? Think of your hobbies and what you do (did) well in school and extracurricular activities. Think of your abilities within the three main categories:
People Skills (listening, coaching, motivating …)
1.

2.

3.

Things Skills (fixing cars, cooking, numbers, details …)
1.

2.

3.

Information Skills (technology, writing, memorizing, drawing, knowing …)
1.

2.

3.

Skills You Want to Develop
What do you want to learn to do well? Do you want to learn another language, learn and like math, learn to surf or dance, or be computer literate?

People Skills	Things Skills	Information Skills
1. _____	1. _____	1. _____
2. _____	2. _____	2. _____
3. _____	3. _____	3. _____

Ideal Work Atmosphere
Describe what you want in an ideal work atmosphere. (Home office, large classroom, busy hospital, courtroom, artist studio, executive office, retail store, outside, in the mountains …)
1.

2.

3.

Ideal Co-Workers
Describe the kinds of people you would like to work around. (Quiet, sociable, professional, artistic, business-minded, smart, those who want to make a difference …)
1.

2.

3.

Geographical Location
Where in the world would you like to live and work? (In a big city, medium-sized town, small community, in the Midwest, near the coast, China …)
1.

2.

3.

Work Attire
What would you like to wear to work? (Suits, casual, jeans and tees, formal, uniform …)
1.

2.

3.

Starting Salary
What is the least amount of money you would be willing to take for a job you loved and knew would grow into something else?

_____ per month

Desired Salary
What is the desired realistic salary you would like right now?

_____ Future ideal salary per month

What skill sets do you have that will warrant this salary in the current job market?
1.

2.

3.

When you are fully trained for your career, how much would you like to make?

_____ per month

Further Education/Training
What further education and/or training are you willing to pursue? (Job training classes, university extension programs, professional certifications, adult education classes apprenticeship, on-the-job training, internships, vocational training, military, community college, co-op program, four-year university, graduate education ...)
1.

2.

3.

Career Fields
Which general career fields interest you right now? (Health, science, engineering, technology, business, communication, arts, humanities, social services, government, international, philanthropic, public policy and administration, education, or some combination of career interest fields.)
1.

2.

3.

Specific Careers
Which specific careers interest you right now? (Physical therapist, marine biologist, mechanical engineer, electrician, entrepreneur, broadcaster, graphic artist, police officer, counselor, teacher ...)
1.

2.

3.

Motivators
What are the things that motivate you most in your life? (A desire to make a difference in the world, love of people, athletic ability, desire to balance work and family/friends, financial security ...)
1.

2.

3.

Good job!

I know some of the questions left you quivering in your best interview shoes. Relax. This first exercise is a sort of assessment of what you know about yourself, your marketability, and your skill base. You are not expected to know all of this now. Give yourself a few weeks with this book, a good teacher, and *Unlimited Options*, and I guarantee you that you will feel differently about the world of work and your place in it.

Keep going…

Exercise 2: Exploring Your Joys

In this exercise, you will:
➢ Learn that knowledge of your interests, personality, and style of interacting with the world can be used to your advantage when looking for work.
➢ Learn that being able to express your strengths and discuss how others see you creates important building blocks for great interviews.

The most ordinary things you do in life tell you a great deal about yourself. By looking at what you enjoy, how you do things, and who you do it with, you can learn about the environment you work best in and are most comfortable with. The following exercises will help you further develop your portrait. You may be surprised at who you see.

> *It's never too late — in fiction or in life — to revise."*
> Nancy Thayer

Your Favorite Activities:
What you enjoy often uncovers surprising things about yourself. See what you learn from the following questions.

✓ Check your three favorite movie types.

Action	Romance	Science Fiction
Drama	Comedy	Horror
Foreign	Animated	Historical
Animal	Documentary	

Do you enjoy seeing movies more than once?
Yes   No

Why?

Name your three favorite leisure activities. Are you an observer or a participant?
1.

2.

3.

If you could, which three sports would you excel in?
1.

2.

3.

Are these individual or team sports?

What part of the newspaper or news website do you go to first? Next? After that?
1.

2.

3.

Relationships and You
How we associate with our comrades often reveals a great deal about our strengths. Take a few minutes and consider your current circle of friends. Then answer the following questions.
When you go out to eat, are you the person in the group who figures out the check? (**Money Manager**)

      Yes   No

Do your friends come to you with their concerns because they know you will listen and keep their secrets? (**Counselor/Problem Solver**)

      Yes   No

Are you the one who can organize a forgotten birthday party on a moment's notice, complete with hats and horns? (**Organizer**)

      Yes   No

Do your friends come to you because you know where to get the cheapest gas, the biggest burrito and the best haircut? (**Networker/Information Gatherer**)

      Yes   No

Are you able to see the funny or odd side of life and then communicate that to your friends and those around you? Can you break the ice in tense situations using your quick wit and funny way of looking at things? (**Entertainer**)

      Yes   No

Are you the technically inclined who can put things together, fix machines, and generally keep equipment in working order? (**Engineer/Repair Person/Techie**)

      Yes   No

Are you the peacemaker in the group who reconciles bickering, arguments, and diverse opinions? (**Mediator/Negotiator**)

      Yes   No

Are you the initiator in the group? Do you want to try new things and go on adventures? (**Risk Taker/Adventurer**)

      Yes   No

**Look over your answers. What do you think this
exercise tells you about your strengths, personality, activities?**

Your strengths? (Independent, trustworthy ...)
1.

2.

3.

Your personality? (Outgoing, aggressive, shy ...)
1.

2.

3.

Types of activities you enjoy? (Group, physical, quiet ...)
1.

2.

3.

As you move through this workbook, you will learn how to use this information as you explore possible satisfying career paths. Come back here for clues if you find yourself stuck. If you had trouble answering some of the questions the upcoming exercises should help you clarify your thoughts. Come back here as often as you need to complete or amend this section.

> *"Life is to be lived. If you have to support yourself, you had bloody well better be doing some thing that is going to be interesting."*
> Katharine Hepburn, Actress

Exercise 3: Careers That Match Your Interests

In this exercise, you will:
➢ Discover how your interests relate to the world of work.
➢ Learn how to match your interests to careers.
➢ Calculate your Holland Code.

Now that your portrait of yourself is taking shape, it is time to work on your dream job. John Holland, author of *Making Vocational Choices,* developed six occupational themes that will help you identify the types of occupations that might fascinate you. These are very broad and are intended *only* to give you a jumping off place. You will be able to apply what you learn here about your work interests to more specific job categories later on. With each of the following questions, circle the appropriate answer. (Y = yes; N = no.)

R

_____Y _____N   Do you enjoy creating with your hands?
_____Y _____N   Do you enjoy fixing things with your hands?
_____Y _____N   Do you enjoy working with tools and machines?
_____Y _____N   Do you consider yourself practical, persistent, and stable?
_____Y _____N   Do you like to do physically active tasks?
_____Y _____N   Do you prefer to work with things rather than people?
_____Y _____N   Do you like to work outdoors?
_____Y _____N   Do you have difficulty expressing ideas in words?
_____Y _____N   Do you have difficulty communicating your feelings to others?
_____Y _____N   Are your political ideas fairly conventional?
_____Y _____N   Are your economic ideas fairly conventional?

I

_____Y _____N   Do you enjoy solving complicated problems and intellectual challenges?
_____Y _____N   Are you interested in science and math?
_____Y _____N   Are you interested in understanding the physical world?
_____Y _____N   Are you curious?
_____Y _____N   Are you logical?
_____Y _____N   Are you precise?
_____Y _____N   Are you persistent?
_____Y _____N   Do you prefer to work alone?
_____Y _____N   Are you task-oriented rather than people-oriented?
_____Y _____N   Are you uncomfortable in highly structured situations with many rules?
_____Y _____N   Do you want to know how things work.

A

_____ Y _____ N Do you prefer to work independently in unstructured situations?
_____ Y _____ N Are you imaginative?
_____ Y _____ N Are you artistic?
_____ Y _____ N Do you have good instincts?
_____ Y _____ N Are you individualistic?
_____ Y _____ N Do you enjoy expressing yourself through music, art, writing, or any of the performing arts?
_____ Y _____ N Are you shy about expressing your own opinions and capabilities?
_____ Y _____ N Do you have little interest in solving problems that require physical strength?
_____ Y _____ N Do you prefer dealing with problems that an be solved through self-expression in an artistic media?
_____ Y _____ N Would you describe yourself as intense?
_____ Y _____ N Would you describe yourself as sensitive and emotional?

S

_____ Y _____ N Do you enjoy helping people solve problems by discussion?
_____ Y _____ N Can you plan and supervise an activity?
_____ Y _____ N Can you teach an activity to others?
_____ Y _____ N Do you tend to enjoy social events such as meetings?
_____ Y _____ N Do you enjoy team sports?
_____ Y _____ N Do others seek out your advice and companionship?
_____ Y _____ N Are you intensely concerned with the welfare of others?
_____ Y _____ N Do you express yourself well?
_____ Y _____ N Do you get along well with others?
_____ Y _____ N Do you enjoy being the center of attention?
_____ Y _____ N Do you have little interest in working with machinery?
_____ Y _____ N Do you like competition?
_____ Y _____ N Do you enjoy leading others?
_____ Y _____ N Do you enjoy persuading people to accept your ideas?
_____ Y _____ N Are you self-confident?
_____ Y _____ N Are you ambitious?
_____ Y _____ N Are you independent?
_____ Y _____ N Are you good with words?
_____ Y _____ N Are you adventurous?

_____Y	_____N	Are you impatient with precise work?
_____Y	_____N	Are you impatient with work involving long periods of intellectual effort?
_____Y	_____N	Would you like to own your own business?

C

_____Y	_____N	Do you prefer structured situations and organization?
_____Y	_____N	Do you prefer defined tasks?
_____Y	_____N	Do you like detailed work?
_____Y	_____N	Are you good at numbers work?
_____Y	_____N	Are you conscientious?
_____Y	_____N	Are you efficient?
_____Y	_____N	Are you organized?
_____Y	_____N	Are you more comfortable being a follower than a leader?
_____Y	_____N	Are you comfortable with a well-defined chain of command?
_____Y	_____N	Do you like to know exactly what is expected of you?
_____Y	_____N	Do others see you as dependable?

Record the number of Y answers under each of the following Occupational Themes:

Realistic _____   **Investigative** _____   **Artistic** _____

Social _____   **Enterprising** _____   **Conventional** _____

List your three highest occupational themes:

Your Holland Code is _____ _____ _____.

Generally speaking, what do these occupational themes tell you about yourself? See if you recognize yourself in these descriptions.

Realistic people are generally active, have good physical skills, like to work outside and to create things with their hands. They generally prefer to deal with things rather than with ideas or people, prefer "doing" to "thinking," and prefer solving concrete problems rather than abstract ones. They sometimes have difficulty in expressing ideas in words or in communicating feelings to others. Their political and economic ideas tend to be fairly conventional.

Investigative people generally prefer to solve abstract problems. They are observant and curious. They enjoy complicated problems and intellectual challenges. They may prefer to work more on their own than with others. They tend to have unconventional values and attitudes and like to be original and creative, especially in scientific areas.

Artistic people prefer unstructured situations where they can deal with problems through self-expression in the artistic media. They prefer to work alone, have a great need for individualistic expression, and are sensitive and emotional. They often describe themselves as independent, original, unconventional, expressive, and energetic.

Social people are generally sociable, responsible, humanistic, and concerned with the welfare of others. They tend to express themselves well and get along with others. They like to be near the center of groups and prefer to solve problems by discussing them with others. They tend to see themselves as cheerful, popular, achieving, and as good leaders. They excel in communication skills.

Enterprising people tend to have a great facility with words and an put them to effective use in selling and leading. They often enjoy persuading others to their viewpoints and are impatient with work involving precision or long periods of intellectual concentration. They generally see themselves as energetic, enthusiastic, adventurous, self-confident, and dominant.

Conventional people generally prefer highly ordered activities, do not enjoy being the leader, and like working in a well-established chain of command. They like to know exactly what is expected of them and feel uncomfortable when they don't know the "rules." They generally see themselves as conventional, stable, well-controlled, and dependable. They tend to be detail-oriented, enjoying analyzing facts and numbers and operating business machines. Here is a sampling of occupations under each of the themes.

*These should start you thinking about the variety of opportunities you have to choose from.

Realistic

- Animal Caretaker
- Architectural Drafter
- Auto Mechanic
- Carpenter/Builder
- Commercial Airplane Pilot
- Commercial Diver
- Computer Specialist
- Dental Hygienist
- Electrician
- Electronics/Research
- Farmer
- Firefighter
- Florist
- Food Service Worker
- Forestry Worker
- Geologist
- Hair Stylist
- Interior Decorator/Set Designer
- Jeweler
- Landscape Gardener
- Logger
- Machine Installer
- Machinist
- Manufacturing Engineer
- Mechanical Engineer
- Nurse
- Optical Engineer
- Petroleum Engineer
- Photojournalist
- Physical Therapist
- Police Officer
- Printer
- Production Planner
- Radiographer
- Recording Engineer
- Sales Representative
- Solar Energy Designer
- Sound Engineer
- Surgeon
- Technical Writer
- Wildlife Control Agent

Investigative

Advertising/Business Writer
Agricultural Biotechnologist
Aquatic Biologist
Architect
Astronomer
Biochemist
Biologist
Biomedical Engineer
Botanist
Chemist
College Professor
Composer
Computer Engineer
Dentist
Educational Psychologist
Electronics Technician
Engineer
Engineering Assistant
Environmental Analyst
Experimental Psychologist
Geneticist
Geographer
Geologist
Geophysicist
Hazardous Waste Management
Horticulturist
Information Security Specialist
Interpreter/Translator
Investigative Reporter

Lawyer
Librarian
Marine Scientist
Market Research Analyst
Mathematician
Mechanical Drafter
Medial Assistant
Medial Lab Technician
Military Analyst
Nurse, Anesthesiologist
Operations Research Analyst
Paralegal
Pharmacist
Pharmacologist
Physician
Physicist
Police Detective
Public Health Microbiologist
Reporter
Reproductive Endocrinologist
Research Scientist
Researcher/Data Analyst
Solar Energy System Designer
Surveyor
Systems Analyst
Television/Film Producer, Director
Translator
Veterinarian

Artistic

- Actor
- Advertising
- Account Executive
- Architectural Drafter
- Art Director
- Art Illustrator
- Author
- Chef/Baker
- Computer Game Developer
- Copywriter
- Cosmetologist
- Critic
- Dancer
- Dental Technician
- Editor
- Environmental Analyst
- Fashion Designer
- Film Producer
- Graphic Artist
- Graphic Designer
- Horticulturist
- Interior Designer
- Landscaper
- Marine Biologist
- Medial Illustrator
- Music Teacher
- Musician/Composer
- Orthodontist
- Painter
- Photographer
- Plastic Surgeon
- Printmaker
- Prosthetic Designer
- Radio/TV Announcer
- Robotics Engineer
- Sales Representative
- Script Writer
- Sculptor
- Set Designer
- Singer
- Soil Conservationist
- Still Photographer
- Teacher
- Tool and Die Maker
- Upholsterer
- Urban/Regional Planner
- Web Master

Social

- Admissions Counselor
- Animal Handler
- Arborist
- Athletic Trainer
- Biomedical Technician
- Botanist
- Career Counselor
- Child Care Worker
- City Manager
- Civil Engineer
- Corrections Officer
- Cosmetologist
- Council Member
- Counselor
- Dean of Students
- Dietitian
- Director, Consumer Affairs
- Ecologist
- Economist
- Environmental Engineer
- Ergonomist
- Events Planner
- Food/Hospitality
- Geriatric Counselor
- Government Worker
- Home Health Aide
- Interior Decorator
- Interpreter for the Deaf
- Maintenance/Repair Worker
- Massage Therapist
- Medial Support Services
- Nurse
- Occupational Therapist
- Office Worker
- Personnel Director
- Police Officer
- Politician
- Probation Officer
- Product Designer
- Psychiatrist/Psychologist
- Public Health Educator
- Radiology Technologist
- Recreation Leader
- Safety Engineer Inspector
- Salesperson
- School Psychologist
- Social Worker
- Teacher
- Travel Agent
- Vocational Rehabilitation Counselor
- Wedding Coordinator

Enterprising

- Administrative Assistant
- Administrator
- Advertising Manager
- Advertising/Public Relations
- Business Manager
- Claims Adjuster
- Commercial Photographer
- Communications Consultant
- Company President
- Dairy Producer
- Dental Assistant
- Director
- Entrepreneur
- Executive Hotel Manager
- Farmer/Grower
- Film/TV Producer
- Financial Planner
- Financial Planner
- Marketing Director
- Fishery Operator
- Fund Raiser
- Health Services
- Home Improvement Contractor
- Hospital Manager
- Human Services
- Home Service Provider
- International Trade Specialist
- Laboratory Owner
- Landscape Contractor
- Lawyer
- Legislative Assistant
- Marketer
- Media Sales Representative
- Medial Practice Owner/Partner
- Office Manager
- Performer
- Private Investigator
- Public Relations Representative
- Purchasing Agent
- Recreation Manager
- Research & Development
- Real Estate Agent
- Recycling/Refuse Manager
- Repair Service Provider
- Reporter
- Reporter/Radio/TV Announcer
- Restaurant Owner
- Retail Store Manager
- Sales Representative
- Social Welfare Worker
- Stockbroker
- Tax Accountant
- Training & Development
- Travel Agent

Conventional

Account Analyst	General Manager
Accountant	Information Specialist
Advertising Manager	Insurance Analyst
Agricultural Technologists	Laboratory Technician
Audiovisual Specialist	Legal Aid
Auditor	Loan Officer
Bank Manager	Machinist
Biochemist	Medial Record Technician
Bookkeeper	Medial Researcher
Broadcast/Publications Editor	Mortgage Broker
Budget Analyst	Music Copyist
Compensation/Benefits Administrator	Office Worker
Computer Drafting Technician	Data Processor
Computer Programmer	Secretary
Credit Manager	Pathologist/Medical Examiner
Dental Assistant	Production Artist
Diver Helper	Programmer
Emergency Vehicle Dispatcher	Proofreader
Environmental Analyst	Reservation Agent
Financial Analyst	Title Searcher
Food Scientist	Traffic Technician

*For more on Holland Codes and matching occupations, log on to
http://career.missouri.edu/students/explore/thecareerinterestsgame.php.

Choose three occupations that interest you from your three highest themes (R-I-A-S-E). You'll explore these further as you fine-tune your focus.

      Theme 1 (   )   Theme 2 (   )   Theme 3 (   )

1. _____

2. _____

3. _____

Are there any other occupations that fascinate you but are not listed above?
List them here.

Exercise 4: Who Do You Think You Are?

In this exercise, you will:
➢ Choose a career consistent with your personality.
➢ Increase your understanding of and communication skills with yourself, bosses, peers, subordinates, customers, clients, friends, and family.
➢ Increase cooperation and communication with different personality types.
➢ Understand your strengths and weaknesses.
➢ Understand strengths and weaknesses of others.

Read the descriptions of the following four personality types and identify and circle which one you relate to the most:

RELATERS

Need:
Respect and self-worth

Motivator:
Peace

Style:
Are slow at taking action and making decisions
Provide personal service and assurance
Dislike interpersonal conflict
Support and actively listen to others
Are weak at goal setting
Have excellent ability to gain support from others
Work slowly and cohesively with others
Seek security and belongingness
Have good counseling skills

Decision-making needs:
Like close, personal relationships

> *"There's an old story about 3 workers breaking up rocks. When the first was asked what he was doing, he replied, 'Making little ones out of big ones;' the second said, 'Making a living;' and the third, "Building a cathedral."'*
> John Julian Ryan.

Natural Abilities:
Creative
Reflective
Sensitive
Preference for working in groups

Learn best when they:
Can work and share with others
Balance work and play
Can communicate
Are noncompetitive

Have trouble:
Focusing on one thing at a time
Organizing
Giving exact answers

To expand, they need to:
Pay more attention to details
Not rush into things
Be less emotional when making decisions

Use time to:
Develop relationships

Want others to be:
Pleasant

Create environments that are:
Personal

Focus on:
Relationships/communication

Write this way: Pleasant and friendly

SOCIALIZERS

Need:
Attention and approval

Motivator:
Fun

Style:
Act and make decisions spontaneously
Like involvement and dislike being alone
Exaggerate and generalize
Tend to dream and get other caught up in their dreams
Jump from one activity to another
Work quickly and excitedly with others
Seek esteem and acknowledgment
Possess good persuasive skills

Decision-making needs:
Testimonials and incentives

Natural abilities:
Experimenting
Being independent
Being curious
Creating different approaches
Creating change

Learn best when:
Can use trial and error
Produce real results
Can compete
Are self-directed

Have trouble:
Meeting time limits
Following a lecture
Having few options or choices

To expand, they need to:
Delegate responsibility
Be more accepting of other ideas
Learn to prioritize

Use time to:
Enjoy the interaction

Like others to be:
Stimulating

Create environments that are:
Enthusiastic

Focus on this:
Relationships

Write this way:
Informal and dramatic

ORGANIZERS

Need:
Order and sensitivity

Motivation:
Perfection

Style:
Are cautious in actions and decisions
Like organization and structure
Dislike involvement
Ask many questions about details
Prefer objective, task-oriented work environment
Want to be right
Can be overly reliant on data collection
Work slowly and precisely alone
Possess good problem-solving skills

Decision-making needs:
Data and documentation

Natural abilities:
Planning
Fact finding
Organizing
Following directions

Learn best when:
Have an orderly environment
Have specific outcomes
Can trust others to do their part
Have predictable situations

Have trouble:
Understanding feelings
Dealing with opposition
Answering "what if" questions

To expand, they need to:
Express their feelings more
Get explanations of others' views
Be less rigid

Use time to:
Ensure accuracy

Likes others to be:
Precise

Create environments that are:
Serious

Focus of this:
The task/the process

Write this way:
Detailed and precise
Businesslike

DIRECTORS

Need: **Motivator:**
Achievement and appreciation   Control

Style:
Make decisive actions and decisions
Like control; dislike inaction
Prefer maximum freedom to manage themselves and others
Are cool, independent, and competitive
Have a low tolerance for feelings, attitudes, and advice of others
Work quickly and impressively alone
Possess good administrative skills

Decision-making needs:
Options with supporting analysis

Natural abilities: **Learn best when:**
Directing/leading   Can work independently
Finding solutions   Are respected for their ability
Debating points of view   Follow traditional methods

Have trouble: **To expand, they need to:**
Working in groups   Accept imperfection
Being criticized   Consider others' feelings
Following   Consider all alternatives

Use time to: **Likes others to be:**
Act efficiently   To the point

Create environments that are: **Focus on:**
Businesslike   Tasks/results

Write this way:
Short and to the point

Which of the four personality styles described in this exercise fits most with what you know about yourself?

Which personality type do you feel misunderstands you the most? Why?

Which personality type do you feel understands you the most?

Which other personality type would complement you in your work? Why?

How can you best adapt your communication to him or her so that you are effective?

Pick one of the careers from the last exercise (#3).
Based on this new information about yourself, imagine yourself, with your unique personality, in this position and answer the following questions:

What career did you pick?

What would be your prime motivator to do this job well?

What skills would you use most in this job?

What would be difficult for you about this job and require extra effort?

Exercise 5: Attitude! Everybody's Got One

In this exercise, you will:
- Identify your attitudes regarding work/your career.
- Identify the influences that contributed to your attitudes.
- Develop a plan to overcome any negative attitudes you may have adopted.

Your attitude toward yourself, your work, and a career is the single most powerful tool you have. How you feel about managing your career determines the amount of energy and risk you are willing to put into your plan. Many of your attitudes are rooted in the messages you received as a child. How you view yourself and life in general also greatly affects your career choice satisfaction. These perceptions about the way things are, are called *paradigms*.

> "Nothing is sadder than sitting with someone at the end of their life and having them realize they had lived someone else's version of it."
> Sam Leer, Social Worker

According to Stephan Covey of *7 Habits of Highly Effective Teens,* paradigm is the way you see something—your point of view or frame of reference. When your paradigms are off the mark, they create limitations. They are like glasses. When you have incomplete paradigms about yourself or life, it's like wearing glasses with the wrong prescription. The lenses affect how you see everything. For instance, if you believe you are dumb, even if you are not, you will begin to act dumb and make dumb choices. If you believe your brother is dumb, you will look for evidence to support your belief and find it. On the other hand, if you believe you are smart, that belief will cast a rosy color on everything you do.

To help you understand your current work attitude, complete the following statements:

My mother's/female caretaker's occupation was:

_____

The three most important things I've noticed or remember about her attitude about work are:
1.

2.

3.

My father's/male caretaker's occupation was:

_____

The three most important things I've noticed or remember about his attitude about work are:
1.

2.

3.

Name three things you learned from these attitudes about yourself and work that will help you be successful.
1.

2.

3.

Name three things you learned from these attitudes that may sabotage your success.
1.

2.

3.

Name three things you can do to prevent the sabotage.
1.

2.

3.

Name three people you believe will be supportive in your efforts to find a satisfying career.
1.

2.

3.

Exercise 6: What Is Your Mission in Life?

In this exercise, you will:
➢ Identify what's important to you in life.
➢ Develop a compass for directing your life.

A mission statement is:
- ✓ A picture of what matters most in your life.
- ✓ A way to become your true self, reaching your full potential.
- ✓ A way of discovering and reminding yourself of your unique meaning, calling, or purpose in life.
- ✓ A complete and concise expression of your innermost values and directions.
- ✓ A personal constitution, a fundamentally changeless standard for your life, which is the basis for making major, life-directing decisions in the midst of the changing circumstances and emotions that affect your life.
- ✓ A tool to eliminate getting caught up in the things that aren't important.
- ✓ An inner compass (rather than a road map).
- ✓ A way to proactively and responsibly live our own life rather than reactively living the ineffective scripts handed to you by others (family, teachers, associates, employers, …).

> *"Everyone who goes to a job he doesn't like is a lot weirder than I am."*
> Patch Adams, Physician/Clown

In order to discover your mission in life, answer the following:

In my spare time I…

_____

In my spare time I wish I…

_____

I get excited when…

_____

I am touched deeply when…

_____

I am fascinated with…

_____

I lose track of time whenever I am…

_____

When reflecting on my life at my 90th birthday, I will feel I have missed something if I didn't...

_____

What inspires you the most?

_____

If you had a week to live, what things would you do before you died?

_____

At your funeral, what would you want your friends to say about you?

_____

What would you want your family to say about you?

_____

What would you want your co-workers to say about you?

_____

What would you want your children to say about you?

_____

What does this say about what's important to you?

_____

Please reflect about what your mission in life might be, and then write your mission statement. This could be as short as phrase or as long as a paragraph. It could include lyrics to your favorite song or could include your favorite quote.

Examples:
"To be my true self and to inspire others to be the same."
"I'm going to the top, broken legs and all!"
"I will live daily with integrity and hope."
"The past cannot be changed...the future is whatever you want it to be."

This mission statement can become a part of your daily thought process and a platform for decision making. It will change and grow with you throughout your life. When reflecting and making decisions about the kind of work you want to do and what you want your work to be about, keep your mission statement in mind.

> *"People generally fall into 3 categories in what you do with your life. You can have a job. You can have a career. Or you can be on a mission."*
> Robert Gagosian, Director, Woods Hole Oceanographic Institute, upon the death of Jacques Cousteau.

Exercise 7: Your Heroes and Passions

In this exercise, you will:
➤ Identify characteristics you admire.
➤ Begin your sense of life mission.

This next exercise deals with some of the key elements in your life: what you value in people, in yourself, and in your place in the world. Step outside your immediate family for this exercise.

List three people you most admire and what it is you admire about them.

1. Someone you know personally: _____
_____

2. Someone you know by reputation: _____
_____

3. Someone you know from history: _____
_____

Describe, if you can, a composite of the characteristics you would like to embody in your professional life.

If you could present our national leaders with your list of the three most compelling social problems this country needs to address immediately, what would they be and why?
1. _____
2. _____
3. _____

If you could present your local mayor with your list of the three most compelling social problems your city needs to address immediately, what would they be and why?
1. _____
2. _____
3. _____

How could you play a part in solving one of these issues based on what you have learned from the previous exercises?

National Issues/Possible Solutions

Local Issues/Possible Solutions

Exercise 8: What Do You Want Out of Your Job?

In this exercise, you will:
➤ Learn that you can't have everything.
➤ Learn that compromise is necessary.

Now it is time to get more specific about what you want out of your job. Listed below are twelve categories of values. Weigh each work value on its importance to you and circle the number that most loosely reflects your feeling (higher number = more important). Your work in the previous two exercises may help you.

HIGH INCOME
Some minimum income (enough for survival) is essential for everyone. But beyond that, how important are the extras to you? People have different ideas about how much income is "high." Therefore, *high income* is not defined here as a specific amount. It means more than enough to live on. It means money to use as you wish after you have paid your basic living expenses. You can buy luxuries and travel first-class.

0   1   2   3   4   5   6   7   8

PRESTIGE
If people respect you, look up to you, listen to your opinions, or seek your help in community affairs, you are a person with *prestige*. Of course, *prestige* an be gained in several ways. But in present-day America, occupation is usually the key to *prestige*. Rightly or wrongly, we respect some occupations more than others.

0   1   2   3   4   5   6   7   8

INDEPENDENCE
Some occupations give you more freedom than others to make your own decisions and to work without supervision or direction from others. At one extreme might be talented freelance artists or writers who may work without supervision. At the other extreme might be military service or some big business organizations with chains of command that severely limit the decisions that each person can make.

0   1   2   3   4   5   6   7   8

HELPING OTHERS
Most people are willing to help others and do it every day outside of their work. They do favors, make gifts, donate to charities, and so on. *This does not count here.* The question here is: Do you want *Helping Others* to be a main part of your occupation? To what extent do you want to devote your life work directly to helping people improve their health, education, or general quality of life?

0   1   2   3   4   5   6   7   8

SECURITY
In the most secure occupations, you will be free from fear of losing your job and income. You will have tenure—that is, you cannot be fired very easily. Employment will tend to remain high despite recessions, and there will be no seasonal ups and downs. Your income will usually remain stable and predictable; it will not vanish with hard times. Your occupation is not likely to be wiped out by automation or other technological changes.

0   1   2   3   4   5   6   7   8

VARIETY
Occupations with the greatest *variety* offer many different kinds of activities and problems, frequent changes in location, new people to meet, and so on. *Variety* is the opposite of routine, predictability, or repetition. If you value *variety* high, you probably like novelty and surprise and enjoy facing new problems, events, places, and people.

0   1   2   3   4   5   6   7   8

LEADERSHIP
Do you want to guide others, tell them what to do, and be responsible for their performance? People who weight *leadership* high usually want power to control events. They want to influence people to work together efficiently. If they are mature, they know that responsibility goes with *leadership*. They are willing to accept the blame when things go wrong, even though they were not at fault.

0   1   2   3   4   5   6   7   8

WORK IN YOUR MAIN FIELD OF INTEREST
Some people have only one main field of interest (science, engineering, business, helping others, writing, art, music, etc.); others are interested in two or more fields. Some insist that their occupation must be in one of their major fields of interest. Others are willing to work in a field that is less interesting; they feel they can satisfy their main interest in their spare time.

0   1   2   3   4   5   6   7   8

LEISURE
How important is the amount of time your occupation will allow you to spend away from work? Leisure may include short hours, long vacations, or the chance to choose your own time off or work schedule. To give a high weight to *leisure* is like saying, "The satisfactions I get off the job are so important to me that work must not interfere with them."

0   1   2   3   4   5   6   7   8

CHALLENGE
Some people feel more satisfied when they expend great effort in solving problems at work. The presence of a problem demands their attention. Are you bored with easy work and stimulated with more difficult tasks? Would you prefer to work on assignments requiring real learning and effort?

0   1   2   3   4   5   6   7   8

INTERPERSONAL RELATIONS
Some occupations provide the opportunity to deal with people. Some people like to be a part of a team and to participate with others. Would working alone be undesirable to you? Do you enjoy the chance to meet people?

0   1   2   3   4   5   6   7   8

CREATIVITY
In some occupations you are encouraged to try out original solutions rather than rely on conventional tactics and established procedures. Are you proud of your ability to offer ideas in many situations? Do you have creative talents that you want to develop and use?

0   1   2   3   4   5   6   7   8

Scoring

For each section (1–12) enter your sore under the column labeled "Initial Score." After the numbers have been entered, total the column. If the total exceeds a score of 48, go back to each value and adjust or eliminate original sores so that the total does not exceed 48. (If your numbers do not add up to 48, you must adjust upward to reach the desired number.) Enter those adjusted scores under the column labeled "Adjusted Score." In a sense you are ranking your values. This "Adjusted Score" should reflect those values about which you feel the strongest. These are the attributes you should be looking for when evaluating any job or job offer.

Values	Initial Score	Adjusted Score
(1) High Income	_____	_____
(2) Prestige	_____	_____
(3) Independence	_____	_____
(4) Helping Others	_____	_____
(5) Security	_____	_____
(6) Variety	_____	_____

(7) Leadership   _____   _____

(8) Interest Field   _____   _____

(9) Leisure   _____   _____

(10) Challenge   _____   _____

(11) Interpersonal Relations   _____   _____

(12) Creativity   _____   _____

Total Points   _____   _____

Adjusted Pts. 48

After your adjusted score:

What are your three highest values?
1.

2.

3.

In what areas did you have to compromise?
1.

2.

3.

Take a few minutes and jot down your feelings as you worked through the exercise.
What did you learn from this exercise about yourself? Your decision-making process? Your expectations about work?

What made the process frustrating?

How did you pare down or increase your numbers to reach 48? Be able to describe that process in class.

Which values were you unwilling to compromise on?

Did you give any of the values a 0 score in the second round? How did you arrive at that decision?

What insights has this exercise given you about how you do things that you can now incorporate into your knowledge bank for those **behavior-based interview questions**?

Keep going…more questions…more information…more knowledge…very soon it is all going to start to make sense.

Trust me, trust the process, and trust yourself.

Exercise 9: Feeling Good about Yourself

In this exercise, you will:
➢ Identify your personality strengths.
➢ Identify transferable skills you already have.
➢ Continue the development of a Professional Self vocabulary.

You have distinctive personal characteristics, and they affect the way you interact with the world and the way it reacts to you. Circle the strengths that describe you best. List more at the bottom as they come to mind. These are the elements that add color to your self-portrait or in this case your **Professional Self.**

Active, adaptable, adventurous, ambitious, assertive, balanced, calm, caring,

charismatic, charming, child-like, clever, competitive, confident, controlled,

cooperative, courageous, creative, curious, dedicated, dependable, diplomatic,

dominant, emotional, empathetic, energetic, enterprising, enthusiastic, expressive,

faithful, forthright, friendly, giving, gracious, gentle, handy, hardworking, honest,

hopeful, humble, humorous, independent, influencing, innovative, inspiring,

inventive, joyful, kind, knowledgeable, loving, loyal, mature, methodical,

meticulous, nonconformist, nurturing, open-minded, outgoing, patient,

persevering, persuasive, physical, precise, predictable, preserving, protective, quick, quiet,

realistic, reliable, respectful, responsible, resourceful, risk taker, self-assured,

self-sufficient, sensitive, sharing, sharp, spontaneous, stable, steady, structured,

systematic, tactful, tenacious, thankful, trusting, trustworthy, unconventional,

unique, unselfish, versatile, wild …

Feel free to add your own list of descriptors:

_____

_____

_____

From the list above, write down your three major strengths.

1.

2.

3.

Cite an example of a time when you have exhibited this particular strength to your advantage.

Strength 1:

Strength 2:

Strength 3:

Congratulations! You have just created three more great stories to use in your interviews. We have a long way to go before we know enough about ourselves to interview well, so you know the old saying…keep going.

Exercise 10: Learning from the Past

In this exercise, you will:
- Learn that experience is the best teacher.
- Discover that there are no mistakes, only lessons to be learned.
- Discover that there is no such thing as unskilled labor.

Here is an exercise to flesh out what gives you satisfaction—what makes you proud of yourself.

Take a specific experience you remember in vivid detail, one you are especially proud of and in which you played an active role. This can be something you did while working, something you achieved through involvement with the community or social groups, something you did at school, or maybe something that improved your family's home life.

Focus on those things that are of paramount importance to an employer—those activities and accomplishments that an employer will perceive to be important to an organization's long-term strategic goals. Employers want to know about leadership, taking responsibility for a project, setting a goal, and bringing together the people and resources to achieve that goal. Don't overlook your volunteer experiences, especially if you prepared a budget, produced a newsletter, designed advertising flyers, held office in student or real government, organized parties or events, organized conferences and other meetings, or raised funds. Don't forget about other activities such as involvement in clubs, sports, youth groups, or performances.

On a separate sheet of paper, write down this experience and describe your part in it. Take as much time and space as you need. Don't rush. Linger over the memory. Pay particular attention to your role in this experience, what you learned from it, and how you challenged yourself in unexpected ways during the experience.

Circle your achievements and list them here.
1.

2.

3.

List any other successes or achievements that made you proud.
1.

2.

3.

Think back on the last three days. List your major activities. Include your school and/or work responsibilities and your volunteer and leisure activities.

Day 1: _____

Day 2: _____

Day 3: _____

List the three activities that gave you the most satisfaction.
1.

2.

3.

For each of the above activities, list the following:

What the activity involved (what your **responsibilities** were)
1.

2.

3.

What it took to accomplish each activity (what **skills** you had to know or learn to successfully complete the duties)

1.

2.

3.

What the result was. (What you **accomplished**).

1.

2.

3.

As you prepare for your interviews and draft your résumés, you will want to remember these three words: **Responsibilities, Skills, Accomplishments.**

These categories will help you break down your interview answers into meaningful, value-adding language the employer will understand. This system will give you the best possible results when organizing your interview information.

Exercise 11: What Do You Do Well?

In this exercise, you will:
➢ Identify what you are good at and which skills you most enjoy using.
➢ Learn to articulate your skills well on a résumé and in an interview.
➢ Begin to see a direction for your career goals by identifying your most enjoyable skills.

> *"Everyone has talent. What is rare is the courage to follow the talent to the dark place where it leads."*
> Erica Jong, Writer

A successful career involves a series of jobs throughout your adult life that increase your skill bank, that is, your worth in the job marketplace. What skills do you have to offer an employer in order to get the job of your choice? Acknowledging the skills you already have broadens your perspective in determining appropriate job qualifications. Having a good idea of what your skill base is will help you determine your viability and versatility in the job market. Most employers will select applicants who can describe experiences in detail and relate those experiences to the job at hand. During the interview they may pose questions such as, "What would you do if…?" "Give me an example of when…" or "Have you been in a situation like this and how did your react?" These questions are commonly used in what is called a *behavior-based interview,* where the employer is trying to get an idea of how you do things. What processes you use to make decisions. How you handle situations that call for quick decisive actions. All of this information will help the employer see how you observe and analyze situations as well as your problem-solving ability. Describing your skills in forceful, job-related terms enhances your ability to convince others of your worth.

The next series of exercises will give you the structure to put your experiences into meaningful "scripts" that will add value to your Professional Self. Although awkward at first, remember that learning to ride a bicycle required time, support, patience, and *practice.* The same is true here. Generally speaking, there are three types of skills: transferable skills, which you carry from one career to another; job-specific skills, which relate to only one or two settings; and self-management skills we use in all aspects of our lives. For now, you will deal only with transferable skills.

Below are a list of transferable skills, categorized into three areas: **data, people,** and **things**.
Check you favorite skills.
Circle those you do well.
Underline those you want to learn to do better.

Keep in mind that, as Richard Bolles puts it, you will generally enjoy something if you do it well, and if it is a skill you enjoy, it is generally because you do it well. Now star your top three skills for each category

DATA/INFORMATION

- Copying
- Computing
- Compiling
- Analyzing
- Coordinating
- Synthesizing
- Comparing
- Gathering
- Researching
- Studying
- Imagining
- Inventing
- Designing
- Adapting
- Translating
- Programming
- Developing
- Improving
- Visualizing
- Drawing
- Painting
- Creating
- Synthesizing
- Problem solving
- Keeping records
- Recording
- Data entry
- Filing
- Remembering
- Administering
- Allocating
- Analyzing
- Appraising
- Auditing
- Balancing
- Budgeting
- Developing
- Projecting
- Writing
- Editing
- Conceptualizing
- Creating
- Designing
- Illustrating
- Integrating
- Planning
- Revitalizing
- Setting goals
- Collecting
- Reviewing
- Summarizing
- Systematizing
- Organizing
- Scheduling
- Improving
- Other _____
- Other _____
- Other _____

PEOPLE

Serving
Taking instruction
Helping
Talking
Speaking
Writing
Persuading
Supervising
Instructing
Teaching
Tutoring
Training
Negotiating
Mentoring
Advising
Coaching
Counseling
Diagnosing
Treating
Assessing
Evaluating
Recruiting
Selling
Representing others
Interpreting
Speaking publicly
Performing
Entertaining
Leading
Guiding a discussion
Producing

Being a pioneer
Founding
Managing
Marketing
Addressing
Arranging
Authoring
Corresponding
Directing
Enlisting
Influencing
Publicizing
Coordinating
Counseling
Demonstrating
Enabling
Encouraging
Evaluating
Explaining
Facilitating
Guiding
Initiating
Rehabilitating
Critiquing
Examining
Interviewing
Investigating
Assigning
Other _____
Other _____
Other _____

THINGS

Playing sports	Preparing
Exercising	Producing
Dancing	Manufacturing
Moving	Maintaining
Acting	Repairing
Growing plants	Assembling
Raising animals	Disassembling
Training animals	Constructing
Handling	Reconstructing
Tending	Modeling
Manipulating	Remodeling
Driving	Assembling
Operating	Building
Doing precision work	Engineering
Setting up	Operating
Playing instruments	Overhauling
Eye-hand coordinating	Upgrading
Working with tools	Extracting
Crafting	Identifying
Shaping	Consolidating
Painting	Other _____
Restoring	Other _____
Cleaning	Other _____

Review your identified skills.

Now go back to Exercise 3. How do these skills relate to your Holland Occupational Themes? (R-I-A-S-E-C)?

Do they confirm or broaden your interests? Confirm _____ Broaden _____

Exercise 12: How Do Your "Smarts" Work?

In this exercise, you will:
➢ Identify the ways you learn best.
➢ Increase your self-esteem by realizing you are already smart.

What is the easiest way for you to learn? By doing or by reading and listening to a lecture, by interacting with others, or by thinking it through on your own? By using music, math, language, logic, people, thinking, physical movement? According to Jack Canfield, of *Chicken Soup for the Soul* fame, your brain receives messages in three ways: visually (what you see), auditory (what you hear), and kinesthetically (what you feel). This exercise will help you identify how you learn best.

If you are at the beginning of your career, knowing your areas of strongest intelligence will help you choose a school or training program that teaches the way you learn. For example, some universities are theory or research based, some emphasize a more practical approach, and some schools specialize in the hands-on approach. It will also help you choose a major in college that complements the way you learn. In the career planning process it will help you choose careers that make the most of your learning styles.

The following checklist will help you understand yourself and plan for developing your competencies in the workplace.

Learning Styles Checklist

STYLE ONE:

Y _____ N _____ I learn easily from books.

Y _____ N _____ I learn a lot from listening to instructors.

Y _____ N _____ I really enjoy explaining, teaching, and learning.

Y _____ N _____ I find it easy and fun to learn a new language.

Y _____ N _____ I have a good memory for things I learn.

Total "yes" answers: _____

STYLE TWO:

Y _____ N _____ I am good at solving problems with abstract symbols.

Y _____ N _____ I enjoy working with numbers and making calculations.

Y _____ N _____ I find it easy to deduce conclusions based on available information.

Y _____ N _____ I remember information best when it is numbered and in logical order.

Y _____ N _____ I can easily apply new information to existing formulas.

Total "yes" answers: _____

STYLE THREE:

Y _____ N _____ Diagrams and drawings help me understand new concepts.

Y _____ N _____ Give me a map and I can find my way anywhere.

Y _____ N _____ I'd rather watch an expert first, then try a new skill.

Y _____ N _____ I can decipher information best when it is plotted in a graph or chart.

Y _____ N _____ I prefer to explain my ideas by drawing pictures.

Total "yes" answers: _____

STYLE FOUR:

Y _____ N _____ I learn by doing.

Y _____ N _____ The classes I am best at in school involve physical movement.

Y _____ N _____ I often learn well by imitating others.

Y _____ N _____ I prefer to explain my ideas by acting them out in role-plays.

Y _____ N _____ I enjoy challenging myself by doing physical activities.

Total "yes" answers: _____

STYLE FIVE:

Y _____ N _____ I can learn information easily when I put it to music.

Y _____ N _____ I can't concentrate on my work unless there is background music playing.

Y _____ N _____ I find it easy to recognize rhythms in the sounds I hear.

Y _____ N _____ I always remember songs I hear on the radio.

Y _____ N _____ I can easily reproduce sounds and music I hear.

Total "yes" answers: _____

STYLE SIX:

Y _____ N _____ I learn a lot from discussions.

Y _____ N _____ I work more efficiently when in a group.

Y _____ N _____ I am perceptive of people's thoughts, desires, and intentions.

Y _____ N _____ I learn about others by viewing things from their perspective.

Y _____ N _____ I can easily get information from people rather then from books.

Total "yes" answers: _____

STYLE SEVEN:

Y _____ N _____ I learn best by reflecting quietly upon my thoughts.

Y _____ N _____ I remember information easily when I can relate it to my own experiences.

Y _____ N _____ I succeed most often when I rely on my intuition.

Y _____ N _____ It is easier for me to talk about my personal feelings than to discuss abstract concepts

Total "yes" answers: _____

Now that you have completed the above list and have totaled the number of "yes" answers for each section, read the descriptions of your highest numbers. Remember, the higher the number, the stronger your learning style. Some individuals learn best by one distinct style, whereas others learn best by a variety of learning styles.

STYLE ONE:
Linguistic Intelligence (Word Smart)—You enjoy reading, writing, and playing word games and enjoy English and foreign languages. You think in *words*. You tend to do well in a traditional classroom setting dominated by the written and spoken word, such as teacher lectures, notes, and worksheets.

STYLE TWO:
Logical-Mathematical Intelligence (Logic Smart)—You enjoy experimenting, questioning, figuring out puzzles, and calculating and enjoy math and science. You think by *reasoning*. You are often called a "scientific thinker." You learn well using inductive and deductive thinking/reasoning. Numbers and recognition of abstract patterns make sense.

STYLE THREE:
Spatial Intelligence (Visual Smart)—You enjoy designing, drawing, visualizing, doodling, drafting, imagining, and looking at maps and enjoy geometry and art. You think in *images and pictures*. You often rely on the sense of sight and being able to visualize an object to create internal mental images and pictures.

STYLE FOUR:
Bodily-Kinesthetic Intelligence (Body Smart)—You enjoy dancing, telling stories, running, jumping, building, touching, gesturing, playing sports, engaging in drama, being hands-on when learning, and using tools. You think through *tactile sensations*. Your intelligence is related to physical movement. You learn best by doing and by involvement. Experience aids in learning.

STYLE FIVE:
Musical Intelligence (Music Smart)—You enjoy singing, whistling, humming, tapping feet/hands, playing drums, and making rhythms and like the band and chorus. You think via *rhythms and melodies*. Your intelligence is based on the recognition of tonal patterns, including various environmental sounds, and on a sensitivity to rhythm and beats.

STYLE SIX:
Interpersonal Intelligence (People Smart)—You enjoy leading, organizing, relating, influencing, mediating, attending parties, and talking. You think by *bouncing ideas off other people.* You tend to learn well through interacting and communicating with others. You value and learn from others' opinions and prefer to study with at least one other person.

STYLE SEVEN:
Intrapersonal Intelligence (Self Smart)—You enjoy setting goals, dreaming, thinking, being quiet, planning, and being alone. You think deeply *inside yourself.* You prefer to get work done alone using self-reflection and your own thoughts and ideas.

To learn more about Howard Gardner's Theory of Multiple Intelligences, check out these websites:
http://www.america-tomorrow.com/ati/nhl80402.htm
http://www.ndcrn.com/students/planning/doc/understand-yourself.rtf

"It is not a matter of if you are smart; it is a matter of how you are smart"
                                                                    Jenny Erickson Cooper

Exercise 13: Imagining Your Ideal Career

In this exercise, you will:
➢ Picture your ideal career.
➢ Look at the particulars you want in your ideal career.

Another way of identifying what you want out of life is to daydream about your perfect job. In this day and age, it is getting more and more difficult to be alone with one's thoughts. Everyone seems to be plugged into some sort of device. Everywhere you go, people are listening to sounds from computers, iPods, cell phones—you name it. If it has earplugs, someone will listen to it. With all the chatter and sounds hitting us every day, it is becoming obsolete to actually sit quietly alone with one's thoughts. In this next exercise, that is exactly what I am asking you to do. You will be surprised at how hard it is to do, but the clarity you experience may well be worth the false starts you may experience the first couple of times you try this. Hang in there and follow the directions as closely as possible.

Henrietta Sparks, in her book *Career Choice, Career Change, Career Success: Imagination at Work* suggests you try this. Find 20 minutes when you will not be interrupted. Find a quiet spot and a timer. Set the timer for 20 minutes. Close your eyes and take a deep breath through your nose and slowly let it out through your mouth. As you continue to breathe deeply, tightly squeeze and then release each part of your body, beginning with your toes. Now relax all of your muscles. Shrug or rotate any tense parts of your body. Gently begin thinking about what your perfect working day would be like, hour by hour. Since this day is perfect, you have all the skills and experience necessary to do your dream job. You are waking up. Where are you? What time is it? What do you do next? And next. Think through the entire day until you go to bed again. Conjure up as much detail as you can. Go back to the best parts and think about them in more detail. At the end of 20 minutes, slowly open your eyes. Flex and stretch your body. Now see how many of the following questions you can answer:

Where do you live?

_____

What does your home look like?

_____

How long does it take you to get to work? How do you get there?

_____

Are you working indoors or out-of-doors?

_____

Are you working in a large office building? A factory? A small office? A boat? At home? Somewhere else?

_____

Are you building something? What?

___

Are you working with people? How many?

___

Are you performing a service? What?

___

Are you producing a product? What?

___

Who do you report to?

___

Do other people report to you? Who?

___

Are you working by yourself?

___

Are you in a large metropolitan area? A medium-sized city? A small town?

___

What time is it when you get up?

___

What clothes do you put on to go to work?

___

What is the weather like?

___

What does your workplace look like?

___

Are you using equipment? What kind?

___

What kind of problems are you solving?

___

Is the work physically challenging? How so?

___

Is the work dangerous? How so?

___

What are the skills you need to do this job?

___

What kind of education and/or training did you need to get this job?

___

What don't you like about this work?

___

Where do you go for lunch? Who do you go with?

___

What is your boss like?

___

What time do you leave work?

___

What do you do then?

___

How do you spend your remaining hours? Who with?

___

How many hours a week are you working?

_____

How much money are you making?

_____

*"Work is not primarily a thing one does to live,
but the thing one lives to do. It is, or should be,
the full expression of the worker's faculties,
the thing in which he finds spiritual, mental and
bodily satisfaction, and the medium in
which he offers himself to God."*
                              Dorothy L. Sayers
                              Mystery Writer

Exercise 14: Your Portrait Begins to Take Shape

In this exercise, you will:
➢ Summarize your strengths and requirements.

Identify and write your top three items in each of the following categories (refer to Exercises 1 through 13). This will help you identify or create a career that matches your strengths and requirements. It will also help you to clearly communicate yourself to prospective employers in interviews and on résumés.

Interests/Passions/Fascinations
_____

Dreams/Goals
_____

Barriers to Goals
_____

Overcoming Barriers
_____

Personality
_____

Skills:

With people	With things	With information
_____	_____	_____
_____	_____	_____
_____	_____	_____

Skills you want to develop
_____

Values
_____

Motivators
_____

Work Attire
_____

Learning Style
_____

Job Criteria
_____

"The dignity and honor which work communicates to people is derived not from the object achieved but from the person's actual enjoyment in the process, that is, from the labor of one's hands and mind."
                                        Pope John Paul II

Exercise 15: Introducing Your Professional Self

In this exercise, you will:
➤ Take all the information you have gathered from the previous exercises, dress it up, and take it out on the town.
➤ Become a spokesperson for yourself.
➤ Realize practice and preparation are essential if you want to defeat the fear of interviewing.

"Tell me about yourself." Does that send a chill down your spine? Rather than groping for a spur-of-the-moment reply, plan one of your most effective marketing tools, the 90-second commercial. Think about the following:

1. What are your requirements for your ideal career? (Refer to the last exercise "Your Portrait Begins to Take Shape.")

2. What interests and motivates you?

3. What theme captures an essential truth about who you are, what you are like.

4. What examples illustrate this theme?

5. What is your personal style (way of doing things, interacting with co-workers)?

6. What distinguishes you from other people with similar interests and educational background?

7. Why should someone do something for you (hire you, admit you to graduate school, invite you to join their board, be your friend, marry you)?

Based on this information and what you developed in Exercise 13, create a short, light, interesting personal statement—a 90-second commercial—that you can deliver at the drop of a hat. Although it is a good idea to organize your thoughts on paper, this exercise is valuable only if you practice it out loud until you are comfortable with it. As you hear yourself use those empowering words about your strengths through stories discovered through hard work and self discovery which you were willing to delve into during these last 14 exercises. Congratulations you have just discovered the beginnings of your Professional Self.

"Your Professional Self is an attitude, created through knowledge, focused through research, and packaged to sell."
                                                                        Lily Maestas

Part II
Researching the Job Market

What are the costs of your dream career and desired lifestyle? How much are you willing to personally invest into finding the kind of work that you are seeking?

Investment means committing in order to earn a return. Investment in your future involves time, money, and energy. Now that you have identified some interesting career avenues to explore, how much of an investment are you willing to make in order to bring those careers about. Sometimes the investment is more than you are willing to make. The earlier you know this, the more easily you can switch to another career that better fits the time, money, and energy you are willing to put forth. The following exercises will help you identify and assess these costs, and which ones you are willing to pay.

In this section of *Get Clear on Your Career,* you will take all of the personal information you have amassed through your hard work in the first fifteen exercises and begin to apply that information to the outside world. You begin to bounce information from the world of work off you own criteria for an ideal career. Now when you read the classified or want ads, the information will make more sense and you will begin to more easily identify potential careers and positions that will be more relevant and conducive to your career criteria. As you work through the exercises in this section information will start "sticking" to you and you will begin experience the "Velcro effect" of being a good *Career Consumer.* This happens when you have increased your knowledge base enough to receive career information almost subconsciously as you navigate through your world.

This next section will be challenging as you force your brain to learn to make the connections between information and how if affects the strategies you will outline for yourself during your job search. You will struggle to fill in the blanks on some of the questions and you will come back to these exercises more than once as you research different careers. When you begin to get frustrated refer back to the second part of the **Professional Self Model,** *Researching the Job Market.* In this part of the process, we learn how to take look at information from a global perspective as well as what is happening on the local level and how it might affect your job search.

The first three exercises further establish your criteria by helping you explore your financial needs by working through a budget that clearly outlines what your financial responsibilities might well be as you begin your career. You will also have to consider the part a personal relationship will have in some of the career decisions you will be making throughout your working life. After that, the exercises focus on how to access information about the job market and how to use that information for your own use. You are learning a new process for using information, so it will be awkward at first but practice, patience and resolve to chart your own course should spur you onward!

Exercise 16: Developing Your Life Budget

In this exercise, you will:
➢ Determine how much time and effort it will take to make your dream career come true.
➢ Estimate living costs.
➢ Submit your career goals to a reality check.

Early in the career planning process, it is important to know what your typical living costs will be. Entry-level jobs in some of the occupations you may be interested in will not support those costs; others will. If the pay scales in your first passions will not support your current living expenses, you have several alternatives. One is to adjust your living expenses to match your anticipated income. Another is to rethink your desired career. Still another is begin to develop additional skill sets that will increase your qualifications and marketability.

Use your local classified ads, your checkbook, your family, or your friends to estimate the following monthly expenses for a single person living in your present community. Do not guess; have a real-life example to support your figures.

Total Monthly Expenses		Hints on How to Figure
Housing	_____	If sharing an apartment, divide by 2.
Food	_____	Figure daily food costs, multiply by 30.
Clothes	_____	Yearly expense divided by 12.
Personal Grooming	_____	Consider haircuts, manicures, health club, etc.
Entertainment	_____	Include movies, traveling, hobbies, concerts, etc.
Insurance	_____	Consider health, life, home, car.
Transportation	_____	Include car payments, gas, public transportation.
Medical costs	_____	Consider doctors, dentists, emergency costs, prescriptions.
Tuition & books	_____	Consider graduate school/student loans.
Utilities	_____	Include phone, electricity, water, trash, etc.
Vacations	_____	List monthly amount set aside.
Gifts, pets, other miscellaneous items	_____	List all other expenses you can think of.
Contributions	_____	Include donations to religious institutions and charitable causes.
Savings	_____	Consider contributions to a retirement plan, such as an individual retirement account (IRA) or to an emergency fund.
Total:	_____	**Monthly living expenses must be covered by what you earn at your desired occupation.**

This figure indicates the amount of money you will need in order to provide for yourself financially.

Now figure your total income, based on what you can expect to earn from **your chosen job.**

Job description:
From the library, a career center, or the Internet (www.salary.com) find a description of a job you are exploring.

Fill in the blanks and answer the following questions:

Total hours per week _____ × $ _____ per hour = $ _____ weekly pay

Weekly pay $ _____ × 4.3 weeks in a month = $ _____ monthly income

Add in any other sources of income $ _____

Total monthly income $ _____

Taxes: subtract 1/3 of your salary from your total monthly income $ _____

Take home pay $ _____

Will this income cover your monthly expenses? _____ Yes _____ No

If no, how can you increase your income? (Check all that apply.)

_____ Extra job (Do you have the time and energy for this?)

_____ Additional training/schooling (Do you have the time, energy and money for this?)

_____ Raises (In today's market, don't plan on more than 3 percent a year.)

_____ Promotion (Check out how likely that is and determine a realistic time frame.)

How can you reduce expenses?

Don't set yourself up for failure. Be realistic. Your cat more than likely will turn up its nose at cheaper food but will get used to it. In this exercise, creating debt by using credit cards is not an option, nor should it be in life.

Some possibilities:
Brown-bag your lunch. Take a roommate. Keep your old car another year. Rent DVDs rather than going out to movies and dinner. Put off having another child. Move to a lower cost-of-living area.
1.

2.

3.

Is the difference between your expected living expenses and your anticipated take-home pay serious enough to make you rethink this occupation?
_____Yes _____ No

If yes, review all the material you have developed and see if a good alternative comes to light. Then use those figures and do the exercise again as many times as necessary in order for you to feel comfortable with the numbers.

Exercise 17: Where Are You on Your Career/Life Spectrum?

In this exercise, you will:
➢ Realize that career planning is life planning.
➢ Be introduced to an expanded definition of career planning as a combination of all of one's roles over a life span.

When you think of the word career, what do you think of? Most people think of an occupation that one plans and prepares for. It is something from which they derive a sense of satisfaction and earn enough money to support the kind of lifestyle they choose. According to career theorist, Donald Super, a more complete definition of career is a combination of all the different roles a person holds during his or her life span. With this definition, career planning is, in essence, life planning. Specifically, in order to effectively make career/life plans, it is helpful to consider how much time you currently invest in each life role and how much you would like to invest in each role in the future.

The following exercise, based on Super's model, will help you grasp this new perspective on career/life planning. By doing this, you will begin to understand the importance of your future life roles so that you can take them into consideration when you are exploring and planning your desired career and lifestyle.

Put an X on the word according to how much time and energy you are investing in each of these life roles **right now.**

	No Time	Half Time	Full Time
Friend	___	___	___
Son/daughter	___	___	___
Student	___	___	___
Worker	___	___	___
Spouse/partner	___	___	___
Homemaker	___	___	___
Parent/caregiver	___	___	___
Leisurite/hobbyist	___	___	___
Citizen/volunteer	___	___	___
Retiree	___	___	___

Put an X on the word according to how much time and energy you would like to or predict you will invest in each of these life roles in **ten years**.

	No Time	Half Time	Full Time
Friend	___	___	___
Son/daughter	___	___	___
Student	___	___	___
Worker	___	___	___
Spouse/partner	___	___	___
Homemaker	___	___	___
Parent/caregiver	___	___	___
Leisurite/hobbyist	___	___	___
Citizen/volunteer	___	___	___
Retiree	___	___	___

Put an X on the word according to how much time and energy you would like to or predict you will invest in each of these life roles in **twenty years**.

	No Time	Half Time	Full Time
Friend	___	___	___
Son/daughter	___	___	___
Student	___	___	___
Worker	___	___	___
Spouse/partner	___	___	___
Homemaker/maintainer	___	___	___
Parent/caregiver	___	___	___
Leisurite/hobbyist	___	___	___
Citizen/volunteer	___	___	___
Retiree	___	___	___

How did your life roles change throughout the twenty years?

Were you able to balance your roles effectively?

What role changed the most for you through out your life span?

Which role do you think will be the most difficult to maintain?

Exercise 18: Balancing Relationships with Careers

In this exercise, you will:
➢ Learn that you don't make career and life decisions in a vacuum.
➢ Understand that you need to consider the input of significant others in making career decisions.
➢ Discover the importance of discussing with your partner your individual and collective career needs.

> *"Ideally, couples need three lives, one for him, one for her and one for them together"*
> Jacqueline Bisset

Sooner or later you will probably have to determine which has more priority, your career or your relationship. Giving thought to some of these issues before they arise can be helpful, especially if you discuss them with your partner. Recognizing that situations change and, with that, your feelings about these issues change, answer the following questions as of right now. These are thought provokers and should lead to wider discussion in areas that are important to you.

If you are not currently in a relationship, answer these questions with a significant other in mind. The majority of us will have relationships in our adult lives that we will have to consider when making career choices. Partners in committed relationships will be most successful managing dual careers if there is open communication between the two regarding the desired outcomes of their individual careers and their relationship and desired lifestyle. Couples should work to set up individual career goals and collective career and family goals. In an effort to enhance this dialogue use the following questions to prompt your thoughts.

1. You have just received an advantageous job offer to work in a geographical location that does not appeal to your partner. Do you...

    A. Accept the job offer and ask your partner to come along and look for a new job in that location.

    B. Accept the job and ask your partner to join you when a suitable job in that location is obtained.

    C. Accept the job and agree to a commuting relationship. For how long? Who commutes where?

    D. Accept the job but keep looking for a job in a mutually agreeable locations.

    E. Decline the job and keep looking.

2. Your partner has just received an advantageous job offer to work in a geographical location that does not appeal to you. Do you...

   A. Follow along anyway.

   B. Agree to join your partner when you have obtained suitable employment in that area.

   C. Agree to a commuting relationship.

   D. Ask you partner to continue looking for a job in a mutually agreeable location.

   E. Stay put.

3. Whose career has priority, yours or your partner's? Why?

---

4. Where do children stand on your current priority list?

   A. Not at all.

   B. When I am established in my career.

   C. When my partner is established in a career.

   D. When we both have established ourselves.

   E. When one partner is established so that the other may remain home to care for the child.

5. How long are you willing to wait before having children? _____

6. What happens if an unplanned pregnancy occurs?

---

7. Money, and the handling of it, may cause more controversy in your relationship than any other aspect. In addition to its more practical aspects, money represents power. It pays to discuss these issues and how they will be resolved. It helps to defuse the power trip.

    A. Will you have a joint account? _____ Yes _____ No

    B. Who will pay the bills each month and balance the checkbook?
        _____

    C. Will you maintain individual accounts? If so, who will be responsible for what bills?

        _____   _____

        _____   _____

        _____   _____

    C. Who will be responsible for maintaining tax information and timely filings?
        _____

    D. How will you decide on the necessity and payment of major purchases, such as a refrigerator, a computer, or a car?
        _____

    E. How will savings for long-term goals be handled?
        _____

    F. Who will decide on the next vacation destination?
        _____

8. Have you thought about not getting involved in a committed relationship until your have established yourself in your career?

What are the pluses?   **What are the minuses?**

_____   _____

_____   _____

_____   _____

What can you do to avoid miscommunication regarding career goals with your current or future partner?

1. _____

2. _____

3. _____

Part III
Career Exploration

Turning your passions, values, experience, and skills into a rewarding career requires research. You will do this by broadening your perspective and looking at old information in new ways. First you will learn how to identify current trends that affect the job market. You will discover these trends just from watching television, reading your favorite magazines, reading the newspaper, and surfing the Internet. Then you will go to more concentrated sources of career information, either at a career center, at your library, or on the Internet. You will learn not only what to look for but what to do with the information once you have found it.

As you search out this information, think of yourself as a detective. Filtering the information you find through a career perspective, you will begin to see everything you come across as career-oriented. You will discover opportunities everywhere. Until this becomes a part of your regular routine, information will slide right off you as if it hit a Teflon shield. Work at it until the information sticks to you like Velcro.

What you are doing to your thought processes takes time, can be frustrating, and requires patience and practice. What you have done in the previous exercises is develop a new perspective on what you have to offer the world of work. Not only have you discovered your Professional Self, you have also developed a strong, authentic statement about yourself, your skills, and what you expect from work in terms of its intrinsic and financial rewards.

Now it is time to take those research skills as apply them outward as you learn how and where to research the job market. Just like with some of the previous exercises, sometimes you will wrestle for the answer or have three or four answers for the questions. Take your time and go over the exercises more than once. Career planning is not a race. **The prize does not go to those that finish first but to those that finish well.**

Exercise 19: Becoming a Skilled Career Consumer

In this exercise, you will:
➢ Learn that what goes on in the world around you will affect the job availability in your chosen field.
➢ Discover that information about the world is relatively easy to find.
➢ Learn to filter information through a new knowledge base.

Because it is important to you, you wouldn't think of buying a car without first shopping the market. You would first set certain criteria, such as safety record, cost, size, and so on. Then you would find out where you can find cars that fit your criteria. Then you'd look for who would give you the best deal. You would consider yourself a savvy consumer. In these exercises, you'll train yourself to become just that, a savvy *career* consumer. Just as you would research what new car to buy, you will learn how to go about collecting and evaluating the information you need to make a realistic career plan. This will be firmly based on the interests, strengths and needs you identified earlier, and career trends you ascertain from information you encounter in your daily routine.

The next section is designed to help you take a look at the world around you from a different perspective. How can your favorite magazine provide you with career information? What about your friends? Your neighbors, the local news? All of these and more can provide you with inexpensive (often free) career information that will help you narrow and strengthen your action plan.

> *"As a general rule, the most successful people in life are those who have the best information."*
> Benjamin Disraeli, Statesman

Current events also help you identify trends. When hurricanes sweep across the South, wrecking havoc in their wake, it also signals a boom in the construction industry and all of their peripheral industries down the road.

The following exercise will teach you how to take advantage of the resources (people and things) at your fingertips. Watch the news, listen to the radio, read your local newspaper and national magazines, log on to the Internet, or use other electronic media. Look for trends that affect the job market. Record what you find.

From what you have learned, identify:
World issues (war, trade, famine, health care, labor market ...)

National trends (inflation rate, Supreme Court decisions, unemployment, war, terrorism ...)

_____

State issues (welfare reform, immigration, school bonds, education, taxes ...)

_____

Local issues (crime, environment, air quality, water, housing, pollution, public transportation ...)

_____

Name an important government policy that you have learned about that will have an impact on jobs.

_____

Name three industries that will grow because of that policy.

1.

2.

3.

Which of these relate to occupations you identified in Exercise 3?

1.

2.

3.

Name three people you learned about and tell why they were interesting to you.

1.

2.

3.

Name three companies (an organization carrying on a business, such as Microsoft, U.S. Postal Service, or United Way) you learned good news about. Briefly state why this news is good.

1.

2.

3.

Name three companies you learned bad news about. Briefly state why this news is bad.

1.

2.

3.

Name three industries (a group of organizations pursuing the same general goals, such as health care, entertainment, government service, finance, international trade, construction, etc.) you keep coming across.

1.

2.

3.

Name three companies within those industries.

1.

2.

3.

Name three occupations (positions held within a company, such as engineer, actor, manager, nurse, or accountant) within those companies that interest you.

1.

2.

3.

In your local area, name companies involved in providing services to these industries. (Your local librarian, Yellow Pages, Chamber of Commerce, and the Internet will be helpful.)

1.

2.

3.

Exercise 20: Researching Career Possibilities

In this exercise, you will:
➤ Learn where to find valuable career information.
➤ Discover the scope of possible careers.
➤ Review the requirements for that career.
➤ Determine whether it fits with your career objectives.

> *"No person who is enthusiastic about his work has anything to fear from life."*
> Samuel Goldwyn, MGM

Please choose one of the occupations you identified earlier. Look it up at your career center, at your library, or on the Internet and fill in the following:

Synonyms (different names or occupations that closely resemble this occupation in other industries):

Description of duties:

Activities involving team work:

Activities done alone:

Specialties within this field:

Personal characteristics required:

Skills required:

Work environment:

Entry-level salary:

Average salary:

_____

Top salary:

_____

Outlook (little, average, fast growth):

_____

Preparation required (type and length of education or training):

_____

Specific educational programs for this career field:

_____

Recommended courses to help you prepare now for this career:

_____

Exercise 21: Surfing the Net

In this exercise, you will:
- Learn your way around the Internet.
- Explore useful Internet sites.

If you have access to a computer, there are many useful sites for researching occupations, companies, colleges, scholarships, and careers that match your personality type. Explore some of the following sites and print out any useful information.

The Career Interests Game from the University of Missouri can help you begin thinking about how your personality will fit in with specific work environments and careers. You will identify your Holland Code and careers that match your code. You can then get information about those careers.

Go to:
http://career.missouri.edu/students/explore/thecareerinterestsgame.php

Also explore the California Career Zone:
http://cacareerzone.com

A great place to research careers is the Occupational Outlook Handbook:
http://stats.bls.gov/oco/ocoidf.htm

Some college research sites are:
Peterson's Guide:
http://www.petersons.com/

College is Possible:
http://www.collegeispossible.org/

For a free scholarship search go to Fastweb:
http://www.fastweb.com/

For job searches try:
America's Job Bank:
http://www.ajb.dni.us/

Craig's list:
http://www.craigslist.com

For young adults go to:
http://www.quarterlifecrisis.com

Career Planning information and articles go to:
Career Builder:
http://www.careerbuilder.com

College Journal:
http://onlinewsj.com/career/main

Monster.com:
http://www.monster.com

Employment Guide's Career Web:
http://www.cweb.com/

Hire diversity:
http://www.Hirediversity.com

Hispanic career opportunities:
http://www.iHispanic.com

USA Jobs—Official Federal Government job site:
www.usajobs.gov/

Quintessential Careers/10 Best job-hunting websites:
www.quintcareers.com/top_10_sites.html

CBSalary is a free salary calculator offered by CareerBuilder.com. You enter in a job title, city, state, and education level and then view positions with the same or similar job titles. Go to: www.cbsalary.com

For Public Services Positions go to:
www.idealist.org.

> "Banking isn't just money-making. Banking is starting new businesses and saving old ones. Banking is helping the right man over a bad time.
>
> Banking is keeping the heart of the economy pumping. If you don't feel that way about it, you ought to quit and become a stockbroker."
>
> Louis Auchincloss

Exercise 22: Exploring Your Options through People

In this exercise, you will:
➤ Acquire the tools for accessing the most accurate sources of career information.
➤ Visit actual work sites.
➤ Become comfortable asking people about their work.
➤ Gauge whether your first passion will fit your needs.

Before making a commitment to a specific career field, it is wise to learn all you can about it. You may find unexpected satisfactions or, more important, facets of the field that you would not enjoy. For example, one young woman was an avid animal lover, but rejected veterinary medicine when she learned part of the job was to put unwanted animals to sleep. Instead she enrolled in an animal training program, which prepared her to work with zoo animals and marine parks and aquariums. Another woman wanted to be a grant writer until she discovered researching donors to be deadly dull for her. There are many ways to get firsthand information about your field of interest. Here are a few suggestions. Choose at least one, but remember, the more you do, the more you will learn.

Informational Interview

This might strike terror in your heart, but you will probably find that people enjoy talking about their work and sharing their excitement or lack of it with newcomers. You might be surprised at how much fun informational interviews can be. Find someone who holds a job in the field of your interest and set up an interview.

Start with people you know. If you don't already know someone in this field, ask your friends, teachers, counselors, relatives, or other community affiliations for references. Many schools have lists of alumni or local professionals who have volunteered to talk with career researchers like yourself. Try the Yellow Pages. Go online for a speakers bureau listed through professional organizations in your area or try the Chamber of Commerce, which might provide you with some contacts for informational interviews.

Face-to-face is likely to yield more information because you will be able to observe the workplace, and this may generate more questions you would like answered, but short telephone conversations, if you are well prepared, will also give you valuable information. This will take anywhere from 15 minutes to 2 hours.

To set up an informational interview, introduce yourself and mention the person who referred you. Tell the person you are conducting career research in his or her field and would like a few minutes of the person's time to learn more about it. Ask if you can meet the person at work or over a cup of coffee somewhere else. If not, ask if the person has a few minutes to talk over the telephone. If you meet face-to-face, be sure you dress appropriately for that work site.

Here are some questions you might ask:
What do you do in your day-to-day job?

What are the positive things about your career field?

What are the negative things?

What education and training would I need to be prepared for your career?

What is your work schedule?

What is the salary range for your field? (Do not ask what his or her salary is, just the range.)

What can I do now to prepare for a career like yours? (classes, volunteer projects, activities …)

What advice would you give to a person starting out in your field?

Do you know of anyone else I could talk with to get more information about this field?

Would I be able to shadow you for a half-day?

If the job shadow goes well, would it be possible for me to volunteer or intern with you? This would give you free help and would allow me to "try on" your career and gain more experience.

Job Shadow
Identify someone in your field and ask to observe what he or she does on the job. Again, you get to see the work environment. Use the sources mentioned previously to locate an appropriate work site. A good way to set up a job shadow is to ask the person you interviewed in the prior step if you can return and just observe what he or she does in a typical day. In addition to the preceding questions, you might ask, "Is there someone else you think I should talk with?" Job shadowing usually takes 2 to 4 hours.

Internship
Internships let you gain actual experience in the field by working at a site for a short period of time. These often are geared to school semesters, summer vacation periods, and other vacation periods or to a specific project. These can be arranged through a school or independently. In many instances, interns are not paid, but not always. The process for setting up an internship is similar to arranging for informational interviews or job shadows. After introducing yourself and giving your referral, simply say, "I'm doing career research in your field. Do you offer any internship opportunities?" and let them take it from there. There are some helpful national and international internship websites that will give you all the information you need to research and apply. You can do a basic Google search using "Internship Directories" and your entry.

Volunteer
Offer your services to an organization in your field of interest. There are plenty of opportunities to volunteer, and a good place to start is at the local offices of the United Way and the Chamber of Commerce. These agencies have connections with most of the nonprofit groups, social service organizations, and businesses in your area.

Although volunteers are unpaid, they are often allowed access to more than entry-level functions. The extent and duration of volunteer work is entirely up to you.

Class Related to Your Career Field
This could be a formal class lasting a semester, an adult education program, or a specialized seminar or workshop or a program sponsored by an industry or nonprofit organization in your community.

The goal of this exercise is to take this job search back to what often ultimately determines the kind of careers people choose. We go back and talk to the people who are doing the work we want to do. What are they like? Do they enjoy the work? What are their frustrations? What do they dislike about their jobs? What would they change? How do I feel when I watch them do their work? Did I think about the work site long after the experience?

People most often determine satisfaction on the job based on the human interaction and the people they work with. The workplace and its occupants play a critical role in career satisfaction, so do not skimp on this exercise or feel silly trying to set up an informational interview. Getting a feel for the workplace and the people who do the work in question is a valuable necessary piece to the puzzle.

> *"One of the great paradoxes of human development is that we are required to make crucial choices (about careers and work) before we have the knowledge, judgement and self-understanding to choose wisely.*
>
> *Yet if we put off these choices until we feel truly ready, the delay may produce other and greater costs.*
>
> — Daniel J. Levenson

Part IV
Exploring Further Education and Training

Which career-focused programs/schools or colleges suit you?

Education, training, and experience are the three keys to getting the job you want in the field you want to work in. These can take many forms. Even college educations come in many styles and sizes. Here you will look at many ways you can obtain the education, training, and experience you identified as necessary in the last few exercises. Again, you'll see there are several opportunities for reaching your goal.

Exercise 23: Which Door Do You Open?

In this exercise, you will:
- Become aware of education/training options.
- Realize that education and training are lifelong pursuits.
- Learn that a combination of options produces the best results.

There are many ways to prepare for a career. The door you choose depends on your career goal, learning style, and the amount of time, energy, and money you are willing to invest in your career preparation. You may focus on one of the training/education options or select a combination of two or more. Usually a combination is the best way to go. Place a checkmark next to the education and training options you intend to pursue to meet your career goals.

> *"Leaving your options open may sound good in theory, but in doing so you delay making decisions.*
>
> *The whole point of decision making is choosing the most reasonable option and eliminating the rest...for the time being."*
> — Lily Maestas

_____ Unpaid on-the-job training (volunteer or internship)

_____ Paid on-the-job training (usually entry-level wages)

_____ Career-focused classes (usually includes hands-on training)

_____ One- to two-year vocational school (career-focused hands-on learning)

_____ Community college two-year school

_____ Transfer to a four-year college

_____ Four-year college or university (Bachelors degree)

_____ Certificate programs through college and university extension programs

_____ State college (less expensive and more practically oriented)

_____ University (more expensive and more theoretically oriented)

_____ Private (most expensive, usually smaller with more individualized attention)

_____ Graduate school (one to ten years of school after your four-year degree)

_____ Military training (before or after your college degree)

Exercise 24: Choosing Your Major

In this exercise, you will:
➢ Learn more about college majors.
➢ Identify a possible major that suits you.

Many careers and occupations require a college degree. College degrees are awarded for completing a set of courses. These courses fall into three general areas: general education (such as English and humanities), your chosen major (Fine Arts, Physical Education, Teaching), and electives (courses of your choice).

A college major is an area of study in which you have a special interest in acquiring knowledge and information—an area in which you want to certify your expertise. You will take a series of courses of increasing complexity within this major that will give you the information and experience to perform in that area (such as Accounting, Engineering, Auto Repair, Psychology).

All college students must declare a major in order to graduate. However, declaring a major in a field that pursues your career goals can be a great self-motivator, and doing well in your college career is always viewed well by prospective employers.

The clearer your career goals, the easier it is to choose a major. The earlier you do this, the better, because you can then focus your efforts on prerequisites for your more advanced classes. This can make a difference in how quickly you can complete your degree program and actually move into your chosen career. Choosing early also allows you to select electives that either concentrate your major or expand it. Either way can be a plus.

Choosing an educational or training program can be the hardest and most important decision you will have to make up until this time. The variety of opportunities that are available can be too much of a good thing. You need some tools for narrowing your focus.

Start by looking at the following common college majors. They are grouped around the Holland Themes identified in Exercise 3. Add to these any majors you identified through your informational interviews:

Realistic

Architecture	Biological Sciences
Veterinary Medicine	Graphic Communications
Engineering	Environmental Horticulture
Firefighting	Mechanical Engineering
Landscape Architecture	Military Science
Medical Technology	Physical Activities
English	_____

Investigative

Electronic Computer Technology
Horticulture
Chemistry
Computer Information Systems
Physics
Geology
Biologist
Mathematics
Biological Sciences
Computer Science
Environmental Studies
Engineering Technology
Geography
Psychology
Anthropology
Aquatic Biology
Biochemistry
Biological Sciences
Biopsychology
Cell and Development Biology
Chemistry
Chemical Engineering
Computer Science
Ecology and Evolution
Electrical Engineering
English
Environmental Studies
Geography

Geological Sciences
Geophysics
History
History of Public Policy
Hydrologic Sciences
Islamic and Near Eastern Studies
Latin American and Iberian Studies
Law and Society
Linguistics
Mathematics
Medieval Studies
Microbiology
Molecular Biology
Nuclear Engineering
Pharmacology
Philosophy
Physical Geography
Physics
Physiology
Pre Med
Psychology
Renaissance Studies
Sociology
Statistical Science
Women's Studies
Zoology

_____

Artistic

Art	Communications
Theater	Comparative Literature
Supervision and Management	Dance
Liberal Studies	Dramatic Art
Journalism	English
English	Film Studies
Music	French
Marketing Technology	Germanic Languages and Literatures
Graphic Communications	Italian Cultural Studies
Art History	Japanese
Art Studio	Portuguese
Chinese	Slavic Languages and Literatures
Classical Archeology	Spanish
Classical Civilization	Theatre
Classics	

Social

Sociology	Communications
Radiology	English
Early Childhood Education	Environmental Studies
Political Science	Geography
American Ethnic Studies	History
International Studies	History of Public Policy
Law	Latin American and Iberian Studies
Psychology	Law and Society
Recreation Education	Medieval Studies
Communications	Political Science
Nursing	Psychology
Philosophy	Religious Studies
Physical Education	Renaissance Studies
Economics	Sociology
Anthropology	Speech and Hearing Sciences
History	Women's Studies
Liberal Studies	

Enterprising

Art	Law
Finance	Journalism
Business Administration	Liberal Studies
Supervision and Management	Political Science
Horticulture	Business Economics
Marketing	Communications
Business Management	Economics
International Studies	Law and Society
Real Estate	_____
Dentistry	

Conventional

Office Information Systems	Accounting
Biological Sciences	Music
Business Administration	Graphic Communications
Banking	Business Economics
Law	Computer Science
Marine Studies	_____

List three majors that fit with the occupations you listed in Exercise 3:

1.

2.

3.

To help you identify institutions that offer these majors, go to your local library or high school career center. If you don't have access to a career center, you can get this information by looking through *Peterson's Guide to Four Year Colleges* at your library or at http://www.Petersons.com/.

List three institutions that offer each major, keeping in mind your preferred location, entrance qualifications, tuition and fees, scholarships and grants, and housing costs.

	Major 1	Major 2	Major 3
1.	_____	_____	_____
2.	_____	_____	_____
3.	_____	_____	_____

Send for a catalog or look online and compare the programs, including electives. No one enjoys every single required course, but you are more likely to be successful academically and professionally if you take subjects that excite you and that take advantage of the talents and interests you already possess. The challenges you encounter will seem more like adventures, and this sets the stage for your ultimate career.

> "Over the years as a career consultant, I have interviewed many people—both successful and not so successful—and I have learned that it isn't so much the specific training they receive, but their willingness to devote themselves to achievement and to seize the opportunity that accounted for their success."
>
> Adele Schelle, Author

Exercise 25: Investigating Educational Possibilities

In this exercise, you will:
➢ Make the linkage between occupations and preparation.
➢ Systematize gathering necessary educational information.

From your work in the previous exercises, name the occupation or general career fields you want to work toward.

1.

2.

3.

Using career or college software, the Internet, or college guides, answer the following questions.

What education and training are required for this occupation or career field?

Are college majors required or desired for this career, and if so, what are they?

What post–high school vocational, business, trade schools, colleges, or universities would help prepare you for your field?

If you are considering a specific college or university, what majors are offered at these institutions?

What prerequisites does the school require?

What is the cost of your desired school per semester or year?

Name the kinds and amounts of scholarships and financial aid available at your chosen school.

What particular teaching style is the school's specialty (practical, theoretical, hands-on ...)?

_____

What extracurricular activities would interest you (sports, clubs, organizations, ...)?

_____

What is the size of the student body (small, medium, large)?

_____

What type of weather would you expect at this school?

_____

What is the social climate of the school (intellectual, environmental, political, laid back, ...)?

_____

What is the school especially noted for (excellence in a particular field of study, an athletic team ...)?

_____

List other pros and cons you have learned about this school.

_____

Go through and repeat this information-gathering exercise for every college or training program you are considering. Weigh the pros and cons of each and then make your decision regarding your course of action to reach your current career goal.

Exercise 26: Should You Be Your Own Boss?

In this exercise, you will:
➤ Learn some of the qualities of a successful entrepreneur.
➤ Assess your personal comfort with working for yourself.

So far you have tried to determine who you want to work for. Have you thought about working for yourself? Small business is the backbone of this country, but it is risky. It is said that half of all businesses started in a year fail and that half of those left fail before the end of the second year.

However, there are many examples of people who have prospered as their own boss. It creates the potential for enormous wealth. Many recent college graduates list starting their own business as one of their careers within their working lives. Working for yourself often allows you to set your own hours, and many small business are part-time. Whether it's providing a service, inventing, building, or managing, the sky is the limit on the array of opportunities for those who choose to take this route.

Before you pursue starting your own business, look at some of the qualities needed to be successful on your own.

This quiz, developed by the ***U.S. Department of Labor,*** should help you.

> *"It's not easy to take responsibility for defining your own work, managing your own time and money...*
>
> *You'll need to risk rejection and uncertainty every time you call someone you don't know and ask for business.*
> — Kathi Elster & Katherine Crowley, Authors

Part I

Yes _____	No _____	1.	I'd rather be promoted at my present employer than strike out on my own.
Yes _____	No _____	2.	The surest way to be disappointed is to want something very badly.
Yes _____	No _____	3.	I seem to have an endless sense of urgency.
Yes _____	No _____	4.	When someone I know succeeds at something, I often feel I could have done as well or better.
Yes _____	No _____	5.	It's more important for me to do what I believe is right than to win others' approval.
Yes _____	No _____	6.	Even when I have good ideas, I frequently don't follow through on them.
Yes _____	No _____	7.	I like to work regular hours.
Yes _____	No _____	8.	I'm basically self-competitive rather than competitive with others.
Yes _____	No _____	9.	I don't like to work under pressure.
Yes _____	No _____	10.	I'd be willing to work odd hours if necessary.
Yes _____	No _____	11.	I never worry about appearing to be in over my head or exceeding my capabilities.
Yes _____	No _____	12.	Being in complete control of my professional and personal life is important to me.
Yes _____	No _____	13.	I often find that I have to disregard other people's opinions. They usually don't see the total picture the way I do.
Yes _____	No _____	14.	I believe that life is more a game of chance than a game of skill.
Yes _____	No _____	15.	When something seems to be going well, I often get scared that I'll do something to botch it.
Yes _____	No _____	16.	I like to arrange my life so that it runs smoothly and predictably.
Yes _____	No _____	17.	One thing I dread most is failure.
Yes _____	No _____	18.	I prefer working in a team more than alone.
Yes _____	No _____	19.	When things seem to be going well for me, I feel uneasy because I know it won't last.
Yes _____	No _____	20.	I often daydream about accomplishing something that no one else has accomplished.
Yes _____	No _____	21.	I really don't like working for somebody else.
Yes _____	No _____	22.	I'm concerned that others may regard my ventures as untenable or risky.
Yes _____	No _____	23.	I'm quite self-sufficient.
Yes _____	No _____	24.	I feel that the adage, "Do unto others …" is more important than "To thine own self be true."
Yes _____	No _____	25.	I feel I'm capable of succeeding as an entrepreneur.
Yes _____	No _____	26.	I'm willing to devote the necessary time, energy and resources to successfully start a business.

Part II

Select one: **A**lways, **O**ften, **S**ometimes, **R**arely, **N**ever

A   O   S   R   N

___ ___ ___ ___ ___ 1. When I set a goal I stick to it, no matter what happens.

___ ___ ___ ___ ___ 2. I manage my time efficiently.

___ ___ ___ ___ ___ 3. I tend to become upset if I can't decide something immediately.

___ ___ ___ ___ ___ 4. I resent it when things are uncertain and ambiguous.

___ ___ ___ ___ ___ 5. I like to stick my neck out even if it's not warranted.

___ ___ ___ ___ ___ 6. I tend to trust my hunches.

___ ___ ___ ___ ___ 7. I tend to act impulsively.

___ ___ ___ ___ ___ 8. I tend to become very emotional when I fail at something.

___ ___ ___ ___ ___ 9. I'm apt to drop something I want to do if others feel that it isn't worth doing.

___ ___ ___ ___ ___ 10. I demand a high degree of quality in my work performance.

___ ___ ___ ___ ___ 11. I can easily give up immediate gain or comfort to reach my goals.

___ ___ ___ ___ ___ 12. I try to put off making decisions.

___ ___ ___ ___ ___ 13. I react quickly and well to unexpected situations.

___ ___ ___ ___ ___ 14. I worry about being too greedy or ambitious.

___ ___ ___ ___ ___ 15. I try to complete projects despite discouragement, hindrances, or delays.

___ ___ ___ ___ ___ 16. When I embark on a new project, I become uptight and nervous.

___ ___ ___ ___ ___ 17. It's hard for me to do my work if I'm not encouraged.

___ ___ ___ ___ ___ 18. I'm more apt than most people to question conventional wisdom.

___ ___ ___ ___ ___ 19. When I decide to go after something, I get it.

___ ___ ___ ___ ___ 20. I'm able to easily bounce back from failures or temporary setbacks.

Scoring
Part I
To obtain your score, circle and add up the values for each statement.

	Yes	No
1.	0	5
2.	0	5
3.	4	1
4.	4	1
5.	5	1
6.	1	4
7.	1	4
8.	5	1
9.	1	4
10.	4	0
11.	4	1
12.	5	1
13.	4	1
14.	1	4
15.	1	4
16.	2	4
17.	1	5
18.	1	4
19.	1	5
20.	3	1
21.	5	1
22.	1	4
23.	4	1
24.	1	4
25.	5	0
26.	5	0

Scoring
Part II

	Always	Often	Some	Rarely	Never
1.	3	5	2	1	0
2.	4	5	3	2	1
3.	0	1	3	5	4
4.	0	1	3	4	2
5.	0	1	2	3	5
6.	4	5	3	1	0
7.	0	1	3	4	2
8.	1	2	4	5	3
9.	0	1	2	4	5
10.	4	5	2	1	0
11.	4	5	2	1	0
12.	0	1	2	5	4
13	4	5	2	1	0
14.	0	1	2	3	5
15.	5	4	3	1	0
16.	0	1	3	4	2
17.	0	1	3	5	4
18.	4	5	3	1	0
19.	4	5	3	1	0
20.	4	5	3	1	0

Total Part I: _____
Total Part II: _____

Add the totals of Parts I and II.

Total points _____

If you scored above 152 points, you have the key characteristics and competencies to be successful as an entrepreneur. If you scored between 119 and 151, you have some critical entrepreneurial characteristics but not all of them. If you are determined to start a business, take steps to compensate for any deficiencies in your temperament. If you scored below 119, you are probably more comfortable working for someone else.

Part V
Developing Your Marketing Tools

How do you get the work you want?

The purpose of all of the previous exercises was to create the database from which to develop successful marketing tools. The product you are marketing is you. In this section you will learn how to add value to your candidacy for the job you want. You'll learn how to dress up your raw data to showcase yourself as a star performer and you will feel the power of your Professional Self.

This is where we begin to combine the data from your personal assessment with the research you have done on the job market and use that information to write winning résumés for the jobs you will be applying for. You will also be asked to practice your answers to common interview questions to determine your ability to articulate those skills and experiences you so carefully unearthed in your first couple of exercises in this workbook.

This section is where your Professional Self takes on form, dimension, and density. Your résumé will provide skills and experiences that get the attention of employers during that all important de-selection process. You will learn how to verbalize your skills through the use of behavior-based interviewing strategies that help you build stories around your skills to give the employer an idea of your personality and behavioral characteristics.

Exercise 27: Creating Résumés That Get a Response

In this exercise, you will:
➢ Gather the data you need to create a résumé that is industry and job specific.
➢ Develop an effective marketing tool based on this information.

The job of a résumé is to get you an interview. In order for it to do its job, it must convince the reader you have something to offer. You have four things to sell: your education, your personality and character, your related work experience, and your skills. Customizing résumés has become a simple task using the skills bank you have created. By cutting and pasting different aspects of your Professional Self to suit each individual application, you can customize each résumé.

Start now by choosing a job in a company you identified in the previous exercises. With that job and company in mind, complete the following using the material you developed earlier:

> *"Instead of a static list of titles held and positions occupied, your marketing brochure brings to life the skills you've mastered, the projects you've delivered, the brambles you can take credit for. And like any good marketing brochure yours needs constant updating to reflect the growth— breadth and depth— of brand you."*
> Tom Peters, Author

What paid experience do you have in this area? What did you accomplish?
Use specifics: numbers, dollars, names, awards.

1. _____
2. _____
3. _____

What volunteer experiences have you had in this area? What did you accomplish?

1. _____
2. _____
3. _____

What classes have you taken that relate to this job? What did you accomplish?

1. _____
2. _____
3. _____

What other skills and experience do you bring to the table, especially any that relate to the problems/challenges this industry/company is facing?

1. _____

2. _____

3. _____

If you were interviewing someone for this position, what sort of person would you be looking for?

1. _____

2. _____

3. _____

Using the information above, explain why you meet these qualifications.

1. _____

2. _____

3. _____

The following are two résumé formats. Each is appropriate in a different situation. The *chronological résumé* is also called the standard résumé. It lists pertinent work experience in order, beginning with the most recent, and covers four to five positions (no more than ten years). You express your abilities and skills under the duties for each position.

Consider using this format:
- When the name of your last employer is important.
- When staying in the same field as a prior job.
- When your job history shows real growth and development.
- When prior titles are impressive.
- In highly traditional fields such as education, government, and so on.

Lewis McGinnis

8722 El Colegio Road, #108
Isla Vista, CA, 93117

(805) 000-6720
xxxxxxxx@ccc.com

OBJECTIVE:
Entry-level advertising position in account services using sales and creative abilities.

EXPERIENCE:
Advertising Intern — ABC Advertisers, Santa Barbara, CA, 9/2007 to present.
- Designed flyers, brochures, logos, and related materials.
- Collaborated with clients to redesign material using an original format.
- Customized a working invoice and ledger system in accordance with executive management criteria.

Sales Representative — University Directories, Los Angeles, CA, Summer 2007.
- Received comprehensive training in sales and advertising.
- Prepared and delivered presentations to business owners using PowerPoint.
- Developed and prepared promotional packets.
- Created ads for clients and colleagues.
- Organized and implemented original business plan.
- Achieved "Top Salesperson" for Los Angeles area.

University of California, Santa Barbara, CA
Chairperson/Public Relations Officer — Latino Business Association, Summer of 2006.
- Created logo and letterhead.
- Scheduled speakers and companies for tours and conferences.
- Actively involved in projects including advertising and fund-raising.
- Provided leadership and motivation to 25 original members.
- Through active recruitment and educational programs was able to increase membership to 48 students by years end.
- Organized and led meetings; encouraged participation, oversaw all aspects of club activities.

Career Peer Advisor — Counseling and Career Services, Academic Year 2007–08
- Assessed students' needs and assisted them in career development.
- Developed effective teamwork skills through weekly meetings and special projects.
- Worked with hundreds of employers during seven annual job fairs sponsored by our office.

EDUCATION:
Bachelor of Arts
Major: English, GPA: 3.0
Minor: Media Arts

University of California, Santa Barbara
December 2008

Education Abroad Program
University of Leeds, Leeds, U.K.
Major: English Literature, GPA: 3.4

2004–05

SPECIAL SKILLS:
Application competencies: PageMaker, MS Word, Excel, Aldus
Languages: Read, write, and speak Spanish.

REFERENCES:
Available upon request.

The *functional-combination résumé* allows you to be more flexible and creative in selling yourself to your prospective employer. The focus is on your pertinent skills and achievements. Do this by placing a special section, Professional Skills, under the job objective to show your abilities and skills appropriate for the position you are seeking.

Consider using this format:
- When you have little or no (directly) related experience.
- When changing careers.
- When first entering the job market.
- When reentering the job market after a long absence.
- When you want to focus on particular skills or achievements.

Ellie Fairchild

125 E. Oak Street
San Francisco, CA 94592
415-000-5151
ebfairchild@XXX.CCC

CAREER OBJECTIVE:
An entry-level position with a radio station as an On-Air Personality providing an opportunity to utilize proven communication and organizational skills.

SIGNIFICANT SKILLS:
Radio/Technical Skills:
Four years of experience as an undergraduate working at a campus radio station. Responsibilities provided an opportunity to conduct on-air interviews on a variety of topics of interest to the campus community, format musical sequences, program news breaks, and provide technical assistance in the overall production and operation of a 24-hour station. Anchored a two-hour call-in programs featuring comments from listening audience as well as music. Ratings remained consistently high.

Programming/Performance:
For two years, owned and operated a part-time disc jockey business. Contracts ranged from outrageous to the somber, from pre-teens to retirees. Met with clients, developed the play list, and provided additional entertainment during events involving audience participation. In first two months, paid off initial equipment investment and consistently remained booked with referrals and repeat customers.

Communication Skills:
Throughout professional career have been responsible for the preparation and presentation of departmental annual reports to Regional Manager. Effectively communicated budget and personnel needs of department to supervisors,
resulting in increases in both areas. Performance appraisals over a three-year period consistently ranked communication skills as superior. Have demonstrated ability to think under pressure and put people at ease, while communicating detailed information in an educational as well as entertaining and highly amusing manner.

Management Skills:
Successfully managed Handbag and Accessories Department for a national department store located in the Bay Area. Responsible for all aspects of personnel, budget, and sales for a department with annual sales of $250,000. Was promoted to department manager after completion of sales promotion, which increased sales by 15% over a two-month period. Demonstrated strong commitment to team approach and welcomed comments from staff regarding management style. Through effective reporting, departmental sales output resulted in bonuses for staff.

EXPERIENCE HISTORY:
KCSB Radio Station, University of California, Santa Barbara, CA, 4 years
Macy's Department Store, San Francisco, CA, 3 years
Traveling Melodies DJ Services, San Francisco, CA, 2 years

EDUCATION & TRAINING:
Bachelor of Arts   University of California, Santa Barbara
Major: Communication   June 2005
Minor: African American Studies
Applicable Course Work:
- Fundamentals of Acting
- Voice Laboratory
- Social Aspects of Behavior
- Human Information Processing
- Principles of Communication and Language
- Contemporary Am. Jazz
- Hip/Hop Social Commentary
- African American Literature
- Public Speaking

Macy's Department Store   San Francisco, CA
Executive Training Program   July 2005

AWARDS & HONORS:
American Association of University Women, Undergraduate Scholarship Recipient, 2 consecutive years
Macy's Circle of Excellence Award, 2006
Girls Clubs of America, Certificate of Appreciation for Outstanding Volunteer Service, 2006

HOBBIES & INTERESTS:
Competitive running and cycling, coaching girls tennis, and writing short stories.

Audition tapes and References available upon request.

Exercise 28: Correspondence That Sells

In this exercise, you will:
➤ Put together effective letters that make their point.
➤ Use correspondence as a marketing tool.

Effective letters and emails are pivotal job marketing tools. The written message gives the potential employer an insight into how you communicate, organize, and present your thoughts. Two of the most common letters are cover letters and thank-you letters.

Applicant's Address
Date of Letter

Employer's Name, Title
Address

Dear:

Opening Paragraph: State why you are writing, name the position or type of work for which you are applying, and mention how you heard of the opening or organization.

> *"That which we persist in doing becomes easier—not that the nature of the task has changed, but our ability to do it has increased."*
> — Ralph Waldo Emerson, Essayist

Middle Paragraph(s): Explain why you are interested in working for this employer and specify your reasons for desiring this type of work. This is the place for your COMPLETE skill phrases. Emphasize skills or abilities you have that relate to the job for which you are applying. Be sure to do this in a confident manner and remember that the reader will view your letter of application as an example of your writing skills.

Closing Paragraph: You may refer the reader to your enclosed résumé (which gives a summary of your qualifications) or whatever media you are using to illustrate your training, interests, and experience. Have an appropriate closing to pave the way for the interview by indicating the action or steps you will take to initiate an interview date.

Closing Salutation,

Your name typed

Dear Ms. Miller:

As a recent graduate from the University of New Mexico with a double major in Journalism and Native American Studies, I am seeking a position that will utilize my academic and practical experience. I believe the position you mentioned in the Los Angeles Times 10/22/07 article provides for such an opportunity.

As my résumé indicates, I have held a variety of positions writing for the university newspaper as well as professional internship experience with the Los Angeles Times. My interest in working with the Bureau of Indian Affairs and specifically Corporate Communications came after tracking a story for the LA Times in which you highlighted the work being done by your department in linking major corporations with Native American Nations in the preservation of historical artifacts. I believe my credentials will be of interest to you.

I have enclosed a copy of my résumé for your review and look forward to the possibility of employment with you. I will call your office on Monday. I would like to schedule a meeting with you on Thursday or Friday, if that would be convenient. I look forward to our time together.

Sincerely,
Lucille Anderson

Enclosure

Think of a current occasion where a thank-you letter would be appropriate. Write a brief note letting them know you appreciate their time and efforts in your behalf. Refer to something specific about the encounter: tell them what their advice resulted in and the part they played in making your job search successful, expand on an interview response, and highlight one of two major points of an interview.

Dear Mr. Powell:

I would like to take a minute of your time to thank you for the interview for the graphic design position with your firm last Monday. As a result of our discussion I am more certain than ever that there is a place for me at Melmen Advertising.

Sincerely,
Barbara Bailey

Exercise 29: Interviewing for Success

In this exercise, you will:
- Categorize the information you need for an interview.
- Anticipate questions you might be asked.
- Verbally articulate your strengths and skills as they apply to the open position.

> *"The person who gets the job offer is not always the most qualified, but rather the one best able to articulate their qualifications for the job."*
> — Lorelei Snyder, Author

The object of the job interview is to get you a job offer. It is the most important step in the job-seeking process. It allows the employer to ask you questions and to answer any questions you might have. It gives the employer the opportunity to assess your potential and to determine whether you are the best qualified candidate and whether the company will benefit from your employment.

Interviewers do not always seek specific answers to the questions they ask. Sometimes they are looking at your problem-solving style or how you handle stress. They are looking for clues about how you make decisions, work with people, and handle criticism. These are called **behavior-based interviews.**

Once you have been invited to interview, note the time and place of the interview as well as the name and title of the interviewer. Dress appropriately, arrive early, and bring a résumé with you. Have a pen, a driver's license, proof of citizenship, and/or a work permit with you. Treat everyone in the office with respect. Each person you meet has the power to say something good or bad about you to your interviewer. Psych yourself up—have a positive attitude and be yourself.

In preparing for an interview you will want to review what you learned about the organization and its challenges, which you discovered in Exercise 20, and review relevant experiences and accomplishments you identified in Exercise 10 and the necessary skills you identified in Exercise 11.

You should also be prepared for some commonly asked questions. Although no one will ask you all of these, and some won't ask any, you'll go into the interview with more confidence if you know you can answer any of them. Write out your answers so you can refer to and revise them.

What have you done in the past year to improve yourself?

_____

How has your education prepared you for this job?

_____

What factors in your past have contributed most to your development?

_____

What factors would you say may have been handicaps in preventing you from moving ahead more quickly?

_____

Does your employer know you are planning to leave and may we contact them?

___

Why do you want to leave your present position?

___

Why do you want to change fields now?

___

What did you like best about your old job?

___

What did you like least?

___

How does your previous experience prepare you for this job?

___

Tell me about yourself.

___

How did you choose this line of work?

___

Why do you think you are the best person for this job?

___

What are three of your strongest points?

___

___

___

What are three of your weakest points?

___

___

___

What was your salary in your previous position?

___

What are your salary requirements?

___

How did you arrive at that figure?

___

What are your professional five-year goals?

___

Will travel be a problem for you? Would you be willing to relocate?

___

If you are hired, how do you visualize your future with this company?

___

How do you think you would fit into our operations?

___

Why do you want to work for us?

___

What can you do for us?

___

What do you know about our company?

___

How would you solve this problem of ours?

___

Do you have any questions?

___

During the interview, devote all your attention to the interviewer. The interviewer will probably begin by telling you a little about the company and what the job is. Answer all questions fully and completely and use this opportunity to sell yourself. Think about the skills and experience you identified earlier.

Be brief and specific as you communicate the information you feel the interviewer needs to know about you. Stress positive, strong points about yourself but do not volunteer information. Be enthusiastic and speak clearly.

Body language is 90 percent of communication. Good eye contact is very important. Be honest—your sincerity will show. Ask at least one or two positive questions about the company, based on your previous research or what you have learned from the interview. Save questions regarding salary and benefits until you have been offered the job.

Here are some questions you might ask.
- How would you describe a typical day on the job?
- What kind of training can I expect in the first three months?
- When will the first job performance evaluation take place?
- How will my job performance be evaluated?
- To whom would I report?

- Will I have a chance to meet people who would be my co-workers?
- May I talk with other members of the staff?
- What is the career path in this job? What is the next move for the person who is successful in the job for which you are being interviewed?
- Is this a new position?
- What do you consider ideal experience for this job?

- Is there anything unusually demanding about the job I should know about?
- Could you tell me about the people with whom I would be dealing?
- What are the primary results you would like to see me produce?
- Is there anything else I can tell you about my qualifications?
- May I check back with you on [day of the week]?

- Can you give me an idea of when you expect to make a decision?
- Is there a reason this position is not being filled internally?
- What could be my first assignment?
- What abilities do you consider primary to success in this position?
- How will my training be structured?

- Who will do it?
- When?
- How often?
- How often will I be evaluated?

At the close of the interview, state your interest in getting the job. Thank the interviewer for his or her time, smile, and shake hands. As soon as you can, make notes of what happened, both the good and what you wish you had done better. Then write that thank-you note!

Part VI
Goal Setting & Review

What is your strategy for reaching your goals?

Soul searching, self-assessment, and career research are a waste of time unless you put that information to work for you. Like anything else, you will reach your goal faster if you make a plan and take action. First check to see you have completed all the exercises to the best of your ability. Then make a plan and take your show on the road. Who knows? You could be a star!

Whatever happens, you will have made some incredible strides in your life's quest for self-knowledge and control over your career.

> "There is a lot of evidence to suggest that when people can do what they want to do they will be happier. It's not the people who work the longest hours who have the heart attacks; it's the people who have the least control over their own lives."
> Scott Adams, Cartoonist

Exercise 30: Career Planning Checklist

In this exercise, you will:
➢ Summarize all the information you have collected to date.

Now is the time to pull all the information you have learned about yourself and the career fields you desire together and then use that information to create your action plan. Check back to see you have completed the following. As you check back, you may find you want to modify or amplify some of your previous work because of new information you developed in other exercises.

Self-Exploration

_____ Your personal inventory (Exercises 1, 2, 3, 4, and 14)

_____ A summary of your strengths and personal values (Exercises 5, 6, 7, 8, and 9)

Career Exploration

_____ A description of your ideal career (Exercises 11, 12, 13, and 14)

_____ The results of brainstorming careers that meet your personal requirements (Exercises 19 and 20)

_____ Collected written and computerized career information research regarding your job description and requirements (Exercises 21, 22, and 23)

_____ Summarized what you have learned from an informational interview, a job shadow, as a volunteer in your career field, or as an intern (Exercise 22)

Career Preparation

_____ Reset your career preparation requirements (Exercises 23 and 25)

_____ Researched schools/programs and decided on your top three choices (Exercise 24)

_____ Applied for school/program and scholarships

Job Search Preparation

_____ Created a résumé and cover letter (Exercises 26 and 27)

_____ Prepared and practiced for interviews (Exercise 28)

Exercise 31: Creating and Committing to Your Action Plan

In this exercise, you will:
➢ Review the steps necessary to meet your career goal.
➢ Create an Action Plan to get you there.

> *"The difference between those that do and those that don't is exactly that."*
> Anonymous

Change comes one step at a time and is necessary at whatever stage you are in your career. You should always have a clear picture of where you want to go next. Although you may have trouble seeing your future five years from now, it is not so hard to picture and plan for your next step. If you are planning for a change, are just starting your career, or are a student, use the career you've identified through these exercises as your starting point.

In order to accomplish your goal, write out a plan of action specifying the necessary steps to reaching your goal. Add dates you plan on beginning and completing each. Following are some of the components of a plan of action:

Identify your main career goal.

_____

Select some steps along the way that may help you reach your main goal. Check all those apply.

_____ Getting clear on a career that suits you

_____ Deciding which training programs/colleges/school to attend

_____ Deciding what to major in

_____ Generating a way to attend your chosen school

_____ Other: _____

Determine which activities you will complete to achieve your main goal. For example:

_____ Conducting informational interviews

_____ Participating in job shadows

_____ Volunteering

_____ Completing an internship

_____ Taking a class specifically related to your career

_____ Talking with a school or career counselor or teacher about your future

_____ Researching training programs/colleges

_____ Visiting programs/colleges

_____ Applying to the school/college

_____ Applying for scholarships

_____ Writing a resume

_____ Practicing interviewing for a job

_____ Writing a business plan for my business

_____ Other: _____

The next steps in your Action Plan are:

1. _____

2. _____

3. _____

What do you need to accomplish Step 1? What skills are required?

1. _____

2. _____

3. _____

Where can you get the necessary experience?

1. _____

2. _____

3. _____

What education will you need?

1. _____

2. _____

3. _____

Put an asterisk in front of each of the above that you do not have.

Review the skills necessary for your next step. For each skill you are lacking, identify how you will acquire that skill (volunteer, on-the-job training, find a mentor, intern, enroll in a training program, apply to a college, etc.):

1. _____

2. _____

3. _____

Review the experience you will need for this position and identify how you will acquire that experience (requesting additional responsibility, finding a mentor, interning, volunteering etc.):

1. _____

2. _____

3. _____

How will you get the education needed for this position (trade school, on-the-job, certificate program, college degree, etc.)?

1. _____

2. _____

3. _____

How will you pay for that education (savings, scholarship, government program, loan, etc.)?

1. _____

2. _____

3. _____

The first three steps in your Action Plan are:

1. _____ Begin _____ Complete _____

2. _____ Begin _____ Complete _____

3. _____ Begin _____ Complete _____

Once you have achieved Step 1 in your Action Plan, use a separate sheet of paper to complete this exercise for Step 2. Do it again when you are ready for Step 3, and so on.

Well congratulations, you did it!

You have spent a great deal of time and energy in this workbook looking at yourself the way you want to be seen as a working person. There is so much more that you know about your Professional Self in terms of skills, talents, values, and ambitions.

Your résumé will be stronger, your interviews will be more productive, and work in general will have a much more positive place in your life because you have learned to be more vigilant about your Professional Self.

This workbook is to be used over and over again whenever you have to assess your working life. It will help you determine whether you are receiving the satisfaction you want from your job. If not, you have learned ways to move to the next step, whether that means a promotion, a change in duties, or a new job altogether. The choice is now yours.

Remember, luck happens to those who are prepared to take advantage of it.

My very best wishes to you! LM

www.ingramcontent.com/pod-product-compliance
Lightning Source LLC
Chambersburg PA
CBHW081355230426
43667CB00017B/2840